mas

Text Copyright © 2015 Sarah Sprules

All Rights Reserved

Cover image licensed to Sarah Sprules for this book only.

Also by Sarah Sprules

<u>Historical Novels</u>
Knighton Gorges: The Curse of Thomas Becket
The Last Wight Witch

<u>Autism/Asperger's and PDA</u>
Looking at stars at three in the morning

As always I dedicate this book to my wonderful husband and children, my dad and step-mum and to all those parents and carers out there who do a fantastic job on a daily basis looking after children on the spectrum and to all those lucky people who get to live on the Isle of Wight every day.

Chapter One

"Okay that's the last box, everybody get into the car." I didn't even have time to turn around and take a last look at the old place, the heavens were about to open and we had a long drive in front of us. Maddy's bottom lip wobbled threateningly underneath her Batman mask, but I had no wish to get soaked, whilst fighting a stubborn four year old super hero for the hundredth time in one day. This was going to be hard enough, without hysterics thrown into the mix, hers or mine! "Come on sweetie, we don't want to get wet now do we ? Let's see if you can fly into the car, before Mummy. I bet you can't do it." I smothered a smile, at the way Maddy scrambled frantically into the car, without realising that she'd just been well and truly manipulated and sat proudly in her seat, triumphant that she'd won the non-existent race. After double checking that they were all safely belted in, I jumped into the driving seat, only just managing to slam the door before the rain drops began pelting heavily against the windows of our silver Audi estate. "I want to go home" Maddy shouted mutinously, crossing her tiny little arms over her body, glaring at me in the rear view mirror from behind her dark and brooding pointy eared mask. "I know," I replied, trying to ignore the heavy feeling that was beginning to settle deep down in the pit of my stomach, "but we're going to our new home, aren't we ?" I employed my child's TV presenter sing song type voice, plastering on a fake smile, as if we were going on a lovely adventure and I was thrilled about it. Cassidy's tears spilled over onto her cheeks, whilst Toby sat staring at his giant map, the one that had our entire route highlighted in red, even though I was the owner of a rather expensive Sat Nav, which was securely suckered onto the windscreen in front of me.

The wipers swept viciously back and forth, barely even managing to clear the screen before it was covered once again in fat droplets of rain, making it difficult to see where the road was. Toby had his earphones firmly pushed into his ears, happily listening to something on his iPad, whilst simultaneously checking that I was following the right route and spontaneously shouting out "left at the next roundabout," which served to both annoy and make me jump at the same time. Maddy aka Batman was watching the world fly past outside of her window, just in case she witnessed evil villains up to no good and Cassidy was pretending to read her book, though her silent tears were falling harder than the rain outside. 'I had no choice, I'm doing the right thing,' I kept telling myself over and over again, hoping with each repetition that I might feel better about uprooting the children from the only home they'd ever known, their schools, their nursery, their friends… and in particular, their dad.

When Michael and I had met seventeen years before, I'd fallen head over heels in love with him and thought we'd be together forever. Celine

Dion's 'My Heart Will Go On,' had been playing on the radio as we'd sat in his old black Ford Fiesta XR2i with the red racing stripes he'd been so proud of and he'd kissed me for the first time. I couldn't believe my luck, I'd met my very own Prince Charming and our future was all blue skies and rainbows, we were going to be like Sandy and Danny driving off into the air at the end of Grease and live happily ever after. We'd set up home in a tiny flat that we'd thought was paradise, but looking back it was nothing more than a two room overpriced hovel.

In time we'd become home owners and bought a three bed semi in the much sought after Georgian City of Bath, ready for the perfect son and daughter we'd planned on having, once we'd established ourselves in our chosen careers of course. Michael got his dream job as a Mortgage Advisor at a local branch and I'd received a letter telling me I was due to start my own dream job working as a Nursery Nurse in a local nursery, not more than two weeks later.

Fast forward two years and I was in labour with our first child. We'd read up on all the books, the newly decorated bedroom was bursting with everything from a Tommee Tippee Nappy Wrapper to a Grobag Baby Sleeping Bag, I'd wanted to get everything, just to be sure, I didn't want anyone looking down on me because I didn't have the right teething ring or some other silly faux pas. Instead of cruising the rails in Monsoon and Wallis for new clothes, I suddenly became a constant visitor to Mothercare and John Lewis, making sure that we had the most fashionable of travel systems and Moses basket blankets that money could buy.

I was in labour for three days, before Toby decided to come out and greet us and in that first moment that I held him I was overwhelmed with happy hormones and unconditional love for my little boy, I was thrilled to be a mother, even if he'd come along, about two years too early. Michael had been there holding my hand and panting with me until he nearly hyperventilated himself onto the floor. He'd cradled Toby in his arms with tears in his eyes and a lump in his throat and I'd thanked God for our perfect little family.

As he'd grown, my little son had been both a joy and a challenge. He wouldn't breastfeed and had insisted on being bottle fed. He hadn't like being weaned and he certainly didn't like going to sleep either. Whilst other mother's children seemed content to lay back in their Bugaboo travel systems looking at the sky, Toby had always fought to wriggle out of his, so that he could see what was going on and more importantly, he wanted to check on what I was up to. By the time my maternity leave was over, I realised that I couldn't go back to work and leave my highly strung little baby all day with a stranger, whilst I looked after other people's children and so Michael and I had our first fight. Eventually of course I'd won, but it meant that we had to tighten our belts after being reduced to just the one wage coming in. Gone were the two week holidays in the Mediterranean, we were hard pushed to afford a long weekend in a caravan in Cornwall. Michael had to spend longer at work to make ends meet and I tried my best to ensure that there was a hot meal and a warm welcome for him, when he returned home each night, though mostly I was too tired to even speak, let alone put a brush through my hair or apply some make up. Our parents visited from time to time, but they were too busy with their own lives to come over and baby sit for us, so we ended up having separate nights out with friends or work colleagues, rather than with each other and we developed our own interests away from each other, which our mothers had assured us, was perfectly healthy.

It was only when Toby went to school that we were told there was a problem with him. Neither Michael nor I had been around other children and I didn't know that it wasn't completely normal for a four year old to be able to read Harry Potter and on his first day of school, I certainly hadn't expected to be taken into the headmaster's office and informed that they wanted a professional to come and observe my son and were going to apply for something called a statement for the 'extra help he would need going forward.' The really annoying thing was that they wouldn't tell me officially what they suspected was wrong with him, but off the record his classroom assistant informed me that he was likely to have Autism.

It took another year of meetings with various professionals with important sounding titles, before my son was diagnosed with Asperger's Syndrome, it seemed a huge label for such a little boy and for that first night I'd sobbed myself to sleep. As soon as we had a name for his differences, I went out and read every book and web page I could find about the subject and joined every online forum on Facebook and Twitter, how could I help him if I didn't know what I was dealing with ? But it didn't really click into place until I went on the National Autistic Society's Earlybird Course, which empowered me for the long fight ahead. That's the thing that comes as such a shock when your child has special needs, everything is a fight. Of course professionals don't like you using that terminology because they think it's aggressive, but it's really the only way to describe it, you fight for a diagnosis, you fight for them to get the help you need in school and you fight for more understanding and social justice for your child, you fight for everything. Even when Toby was in full time education, I still hadn't found a way to return to work because of all of the appointments he had and of course Toby's frequent temporary expulsions from school for various episodes of unacceptable behaviour. The one good thing about being unemployed was that I was able to make the most of all the Autism related training and resources on offer, but Michael still had his job to go to and I didn't blame him when I'd been forced to sit alone, in rooms full of couples, but whenever I'd tried to explain to him what I'd learnt, he was often too tired to listen properly. When Toby was just two years old, we had Cassidy and when she was four, we were blessed with Maddy. When my little Maddy was two and a half years old, I could tell that she was following the same route as her brother and when she was three, she gained an even bigger label than her older brother, Asperger's Syndrome and Pathological Demand Avoidance.

Every time there'd been an Aspie related issue, I'd dealt with it calmly and picked my battles, employing all of the techniques that I'd learned in my training, whereas Michael simply got irritated as if Toby were doing it on purpose and by the time Maddy was added into the mix, I was spending most of the day in tears or refereeing between my husband and my kids.

When we'd first had children, I'd dreamt of family holidays to Disneyworld, but we couldn't even make it to the local park without an argument. Each time we fought, I'd agonised over whether it was still better for the children to have a father in their lives, even if he seemed perpetually annoyed and disappointed in them and after every argument, a little piece of my love for him was chipped away, until there was nothing left between us except bitterness and resentment.

He'd wept of course when I'd told him I was leaving, but I'd had years of trying to talk to him about his attitude and I'd wept enough of my own tears to fill an Olympic sized swimming pool. After a few days, his pleading had turned into insults and that was how I'd ended up with three children belted into the back of the car and the bulk of our belongings already en route to our new home.

Pulling myself back to the present, I listened to the radio, speeding down the A36, following the signs for Warminster and trying to generally lighten the oppressive mood. I knew it wasn't going to be easy, after all, the worst thing that I could possibly do to two children with Asperger's was to take them away from everything they've ever known and all of their friends, God knows it had been hard enough for them to make any in the first place. Maddy's PDA would be raging too, there was nothing about the situation that she could feel in control of and her anxiety levels were rocketing by the day. But living in an unhappy home would surely be more unsettling in the long run and I couldn't spend another day with that man. Perhaps I should have stayed nearer to Bath, but Toby hated his school and we needed a totally fresh start. Michael hadn't seemed all that interested in where I was taking the kids, he'd just started seeing a new woman at his work, a fellow mortgage advisor called Janey, who was single and without kids herself and I think he saw it as his chance to start over again too.

So where does a mum and her three kids go to begin their new life ? In the misery of adulthood, I'd spent many hours reflecting on my childhood and the one place that I'd always been happy was the Isle of Wight. My memory was full of golden sands, cloudless skies and being completely feeling carefree. Whenever I'd suggested to Michael that we should go there for a holiday, he always used to sneer about 'English seaside towns' before booking us somewhere that involved hours of sitting around at an airport. So when I needed to escape, there was nowhere else that seemed more perfect, plus I knew that Michael would resent paying the high price of the ferry crossing and I would be left alone in relative privacy to bring the kids up by myself. I could keep them safe, keep them happy and keep them calm without him ruining everything. Secretly I was also really looking forward to putting clean bedding on my own bed and sleeping in it by myself, without a hairy oaf defiling it with all manner of eye watering smells.

"Mummy, stop singing" ordered mini Batman from the back seat of the car and biting my lip in amusement, I swiftly apologised, I'd been so engrossed in my own thoughts, I'd committed the cardinal sin. "Sorry I keep forgetting you don't like my singing. Tobes am I still on the right road ?" I wanted to get him talking, he'd been studying the map so intently for ages and I wanted to make him feel important and involved in the journey. "Don't you know where you're going ?" He questioned, suddenly flying into a full blown panic that I might actually get us totally lost. "No it's fine mate" I assured him, "I know where I'm going."

"Well then why did you ask me ?" He shook his head in despair, making me feel even more inferior than usual. Deciding that perhaps silence was the best course for me to take, I concentrated on hating the man in front of me who kept consistently driving at least fifteen miles an hour under the speed limit. I didn't want to let the kids know, but we were booked on a ferry from Lymington and if we didn't make it in time, then we'd miss it and have to wait for who knows how long at the port, which I didn't relish the idea of, if it meant I'd have three stressed out miserable children and the angry removal men with all our worldly goods waiting for us on the other side. My hands shook uncontrollably on the steering wheel and I mentally cursed myself for not taking one of Toby and Maddy's Remedy Rescue pastilles before leaving the house. I had to hold it together, if I fell apart, how would it look to the children ?

As I drove into Wilton, the traffic slowed to a grinding halt and continued all the way through to Salisbury, I wanted to scream "come on, bleeding move it" at the car in front, but I couldn't let the kids know I was worried, so I turned the music up slightly and popped a mint humbug into my mouth instead. I'd lost the radio signal for Heart that we'd always listened to at home and tuned in to the local, Spire FM. I was just about to listen to the all-important traffic report, when Toby started spouting facts about Salisbury. "Did you know Mummy… ?"

"Hang on a minute darling…."

"That Salisbury Cathedral used…"

"Ssssh Tobes, please…"

"To be called…"

"Toby I really need to listen to the traffic report mate, please,"

"the Cathedral Church of the Blessed Virgin Mary." He continued, completely oblivious. "They started building it in twelve twenty AD and it only took thirty eight years to complete, which meant that it was finished in twelve fifty eight AD. It has the tallest church spire in the whole of the United Kingdom, it has the largest cloister and the largest cathedral close. It also houses the world's oldest working clock and the best surviving of all four copies of the Magna Carta." His smile of happiness at the chance to impart knowledge, prevented me from saying 'that's fascinating darling, but you could have waited until after I'd heard the traffic report,' so I simply smiled at him, nodding encouragingly "that's very interesting Toby" and sighed heavily. If Michael were here, he would have been shouting by now and as well as missing the traffic report, Toby would be feeling upset and embarrassed and my husband and I would be arguing for at least the next fifteen miles. My heart felt lighter with every rotation of the Audis wheels and I knew that no matter what our future held, I was doing the right thing for my children. "Turn right in one hundred metres…" demanded the Sat Nav and as I'm one of those drivers that blindly follow wherever the little talking machine suckered onto the windscreen tells me to go, I do it. So without thinking, I indicated and turned right, off of the A36 by a huge pub called 'The Landford Poacher,' on what the sign told me was the B3079 towards Landford and Bramshaw. I don't think the indicator had even clicked off before Toby started yelling from the back "Mummy what are you doing ?!!!!" I slammed down hard on the brake thinking I'd possibly run over a small animal and the car behind me blasted his horn, as I narrowly avoided becoming an extension of his bonnet. I pulled over to allow him to safely go around me, whilst he gesticulated wildly with his middle finger informing me that I was a "stupid bitch" who and I quote "shouldn't be allowed out on the roads." I looked in the rear view mirror and caught Maddy grinning at the abuse and couldn't even argue, he was quite within his rights, I had nearly caused the accident and I was the role model of three impressionable young children, so I did the only thing I could under the circumstances, I extended my middle finger and shouted "wanker!!!" at the back of the speeding car. "What's wrong Toby, what've I done ?" I asked, trembling. "Mummy you said a naughty word," chirped Maddy

"Yes I know, sorry"
"The map doesn't show this way. You've gone wrong. You've got us lost. You don't know where you're going and now we're going to be stuck here forever, driving around in circles." Exhaling, I realised that after nine years, I still kept forgetting that I couldn't just do what I wanted, I had to think, I had to clear everything with Toby first. "Actually mate" I started and noticed Cassidy raise her eyes from her book with a look that said 'this should be good, let's see her talk her way out of this then.' Clearing my throat, I ignored my disapproving middle child and set about calming my anxious young man. "I do know where I'm going, your granny and granddad used to bring me this way whenever we went to the Isle of Wight and the Sat Nav wants us to go this way."
"But the map says…"
"I know what the map says Tobe, but the map doesn't know about the traffic jams we'll get caught in if we go that way. You know sometimes, just sometimes, it's best to deviate from the original plan, I promise. The other way's just boring motorway, but this way is far nicer, okay ? Do you trust Mummy ?" I didn't get an answer to my question, but to be honest it was enough that he hadn't argued back and was busy weighing up whether I was right or not. Maddy giggled as we rumbled over the cattle grid, which made my back ache intolerably and did unspecified damage to my spine. Entering the New Forest, even Cassidy put her book down long enough to peer out of the windows at the gnarled oak trees and leafy ferns. Lining the sides of the road were dried curled brown leaves and all around us they fell in a flurry

of gold, brown and orange. After living in the city, they found the forest completely enchanting like something out of a fairy story and when they spotted the ponies roaming freely next to the road, I caught Toby smiling and secretly felt a little smug that for once and once alone, I had been proved right. "You know this was created as a royal forest by William the first in 1079 AD" Toby began,
"oh here we go" muttered Cassidy, rolling her eyes in frustration.
"Two of William's sons died in the forest."
"Thank you for that happy fact" huffed Cassidy, forcing her earphones firmly back in, to shut out her brother's list of 'interesting' facts. "Ninety percent of the forest is still under the ownership of the Crown. Would you like to hear about the rights of commoners to keep livestock in the forest now Mum ?" Eugh! He'd seamlessly handed me the worst dilemma ever, if I said 'yes' I'd be forced to listening about grazing cattle for the next three miles at least, but if I said 'no' then I'd feel like the world's worst mother. Sighing, I heard myself answer "yes please mate" in a sing song strangled type voice, whilst my inner voice screamed 'coward! Now you've done it.' Although the expression on Toby's face was worth the sacrifice as I listened, smiling encouragingly and nodding in feigned interest, a part of me wondered whether it really was possible to be actually bored to death. Hurrying past the low hedgerows, we soon found ourselves in Bramshaw, on our left we passed a beautiful little church with a blue sign standing proudly outside, which read 'St Peter's of Bramshaw' and a whole flood of childhood

memories washed over me like some sort of emotional tsunami.

It seemed all of five minutes ago that I was a little girl happily sat in the back seat of my parents car, excited because the New Forest meant that we were nearly at the ferry and I would peer eagerly out through the glass, to see what animals would be meandering through the trees. Sometimes, if we were running early, my father would pull over at a pub and we'd sit outside in the sunshine (it always shone in my memories) and I would be allowed a glass of warm flat coke, a packet of crisps and I'd savour every last bit, thinking that I was the luckiest girl in the world. My father had died when I was a teenager and my mother and I had suffered without his mediating skills. With my petite frame and large blue eyes, I'd looked exactly like him, except for the fact that my light blonde hair was just down past my shoulders and his had been cropped close above his ears, I think it was our similarities that had made it harder on my mother to be around me after he'd died. Especially in those early years, I think she took a lot of her pain out on me and I'd withdrawn into myself as a result. We'd grown apart and I moved out as soon as I was able, though she hadn't lived far from us in Bath and to give credit where it was due I suppose, she had tried to make an effort to visit regularly for the sake of her grandchildren. When I was in my early twenties, she'd married a wealthy man called John whom she'd met on one of her many cruises. My father had always hated cruises.
"Mum!!!!!!"
"Mmmm" I replied, only half listening.

"Watch that pig!" Stomping my foot down on the brake, we all shot forward alarmingly in our seats, but I'd somehow managed to avoid bouncing off the giant porker standing right in front of the car, staring off into the distance as if I didn't even exist, which was precisely how my children treated me most of the time. "See I told you this was a better way!" I had to sit and watch the minutes ticking by, making us even later to the port with only the rear end of a huge pig to look at, until it finally decided to move. It was either deaf or ignorant, because even the repeated blasts of my horn couldn't entice it to move. Giving maximum concentration to my surroundings, I pointed out sheep and cows lying on the grass at the side of the road, Maddy and Cassidy saw them, but Toby kept looking up too late and then got annoyed at missing them.

We rejoined the main road again, much to Toby's relief, just in time for us to be slowed down in traffic once more on the approach to Lyndhurst, followed by a stop at a level crossing in Brockenhurst, before we finally arrived in Lymington. The excitement of reaching the ferry port wore off pretty quickly when the kids realised they would have to wait a while in yet another line of stationary traffic, before we could board the ferry. It was at this point that Toby started a sentence with the words that always struck fear in my heart. "Did you know…?"

"Go on…" I admitted defeat, no one was going to get any rest until he was allowed to tell us what he knew, so the only option available was to hear him out, whilst I retreated into my own thoughts. "…and Wight Sun can take a maximum of three hundred and sixty passengers, with a total of sixty five cars and go at a speed of eleven knots…" Damn it, I'd inadvertently tuned back in too early. It was quite a skill to both not listen, but to nod and make the right noises at the right time, giving the impression that you were enthralled. Toby did eventually stop talking when the first cars were loaded onto the ferry and the whole platform of vehicles were lifted up into the main body of the ferry, revealing another floor for the rest of the cars to park on. After what seemed like hours and two speedy sojourns to the toilets, even though I'd asked Maddy if she'd needed to go when I was taking Toby, but she'd flatly refused and made me feel like an idiot for even suggesting that she might want to use the ladies after such a long drive and then had decided at the last minute that I might actually be right, we were waved forwards towards the huge white ferry that towered over us.

Toby's eyes were out on stalks as I drove down the narrow gangway, it was a good job the kids didn't know how scared I was, if we were still married I would have made Michael drive onboard. I hate that I'm such a cliché, but I am a really nervous driver, nevertheless I would have to do things for myself from now on and this was just the first in a series of life lessons that I was going to have to learn about being a single parent, something I never thought I'd be. I managed to park though I narrowly avoided maiming one of the staff, as I seemed to get a bit confused over which way he wanted me to go and ended up somehow heading straight for him instead. The sweat poured down my back as I hurried the kids out of the car and through the doorway which led

to the upper decks. The cars still being loaded on behind us, the doors slamming, the sheer volume of passengers all chattering away and the roar of the ships engines all combined to make for an overwhelming experience, that threatened to ruin the whole journey. The problem with having three nervous children is that I only have one pair of hands for them to hold onto and it's also quite hard to get through a small doorway when said children are all hanging off you and no one wants to be the one that has to let go. Toby and Cassidy slid into the little booth of seats, but Maddy stood rigid, with her cape wrapped tightly around her for protection, it wouldn't normally be a problem but two elderly women were waiting to get by.
"Maddy sit down" I hissed, smiling apologetically at the two women who were about to burn their hands on two scolding hot polystyrene cups filled to the brim with strong tea, both looking down at my daughter who hadn't moved an inch. "Maddy sit down!"
"I'm not Maddy, I'm Batman"
"Can you just sit down ?" I asked over the tutting of the two women.
"Not until you call me Batman." The arms were now folded across her body to show just how serious she was. "Okay I'm sorry, Batman can you please come and sit with us ?" Happily, she skipped into the seat. "Sorry" I smiled apologetically up at the ladies, but they walked on with stony faces and I clearly heard one of them mutter, "mothers don't use enough discipline these days." I poured my scorching hot coffee down my neck, in an effort to stop myself from shouting a response across the lounge deck and embarrassing

my children. Toby stared out the windows, silently watching the island slowly coming into view. I knew he was terrified, because it's the only time that he ever stops talking and when I say 'the only time,' that's exactly what I mean, the boy even talks in his sleep. Cassidy was nearly at the end of 'Anne of Green Gables,' which she'd only begun reading when we'd left Bath and Maddy played a particularly noisy game on my mobile phone to pass the time. As we drew nearer to Yarmouth, my stomach lurched and it wasn't down to the motion of the waves in the Solent. This was it now, the island was no longer simply a far off memory, a fantasy place where we would be happy, it was a reality that we were about to drive onto, this was our new home. I just had enough time to get the children to the toilet before we'd need to get back in the car, so I hurried them down the steep stairs, trying to find the toilets. "But I don't want to go" squealed Maddy, as I tried to force her onto the toilet seat. "I know you don't, but just try, for Mummy, please honey."

"No!" As she kicked me in the shins, all I could imagine were more judgemental pensioners shaking their heads on the other side of the door. "Would all passengers please return to their cars," announced the disembodied tannoy voice and I started to panic. "See if you can go to the toilet and get back outside quicker than Toby." Sometimes I surprise myself at my own ingenuity. "Is it like a race ?" Batman asked, suddenly interested. "Yes and at the moment Toby's in the lead, so come on." I've never seen a little girl or a super hero for that matter, jump onto a toilet so quickly in all my life.

Cassidy was already waiting outside with Toby who'd begun to jump up and down anxiously and Maddy took one look at him and burst into tears. "I didn't win… I didn't win…" she wailed as I swept her up into my arms and ushered a bemused Toby and Cassidy back to the car, whilst whispering "don't worry, you'll win next time," into her black little pointed ear. A middle aged, bored looking man in a white hard hat and fluorescent green hi vis waistcoat waved me forward onto the ramp, not realising or caring that he was ushering us into our new life and I was terrified at the prospect.

Heading towards Newport the view across the Solent was spectacular. The mainland looked so close, but may as well have been a million miles away. This wasn't a holiday, this was our home now and I questioned my decision to move here for the millionth time in under an hour. The radio was tuned into 'Isle of Wight Radio' and the kids absorbed their surroundings from the safety of the back seat.

The Sat Nav safely directed me to Union Street in Ryde, Toby had been worried earlier in the week that it might not work when we were abroad and no amount of assurance would convince him that the Isle of Wight wasn't a different country to the rest of the UK. I pulled up on the downward sloping street that was lined with shops and safely got the reluctant and tired children out of the car, with a mixture of coaxing and threats and entered the estate agents. A small bell let out a shrill ring announcing our arrival and a woman in a skirt at least two sizes too small and fire engine red lips, sashayed her way towards us. "Good afternoon, how may I help you ?" She gushed, as my eyes glanced longingly towards the cinnamon pastries piled up high on a plate on her desk. "Umm I'm here to pick the keys up for Hilltop Cottage in St Helen's. I rang yesterday to say we'd be in and my solicitor would be sending them across to you, the removal men should already be waiting outside by now," I gabbled nervously. There was a crackling of nylon as she made her way back to her desk, which I seriously worried might result in an electrical charge, burning the shop down, if it did I'd make sure to salvage the pastries. "What's the name ?" She threw back over her shoulder, flipping through a stack of paperwork and grabbed a set of keys from her drawer. "Natasha Collins." I smiled, embarrassed at the loud rumbling of my stomach.

"Here you are. I hope you're happy there. It's a lovely house isn't it ?"

"Well it does look lovely in the photographs" I smiled weakly in the face of her enthusiasm. "You mean you bought a house without seeing it ?" She asked, blatantly incredulous at my stupidity. "I didn't have the time to come over and look at it for myself" I apologised and backed out of the doorway before she could laugh in my face or even worse the kids could start questioning my sanity and suitability as a parent... again.

Reprogramming the Sat Nav for St Helen's we swept through Wootton, Binstead and Nettlestone, before a sign with a grey type of goose or possibly maybe even a duck informed us that we had finally reached St Helen's. There was a beautiful green on our left, with a playground in one corner and a cricket match was being played on the village green, making it all look like a scene straight out of Midsomer Murders. To our right was a doctor's surgery, which was reassuring to have it so close, when you had three young children and a quaint country pub named 'The Vine Inn' wedged in amongst a row of terraced cottages. "Is this our new home ?" Maddy breathed in excitement as I allowed myself the first sigh of relief, since I'd decided to leave my husband all those weeks ago.

The only blot on this otherwise idyllic scene was a large removal van blocking the narrow, yet surprisingly busy little road through St Helens and four burly men in overalls who looked relieved and angry to see me in equal measure. "Sorry guys," I waved, flashing an apologetic smile, "there was a hold up at the estate agents," rolling my eyes to say 'I'm just as annoyed as you' whilst silently praying that my three mobile lie detectors wouldn't contradict me, luckily for me they were far too busy taking in their new surroundings to pay any attention to what I was saying.

With the help of four men who clearly couldn't wait to offload the lorry so they could get back on the ferry and back to Bath, we managed to have everything safely stowed in our new home within an hour. Hilltop Cottage was everything I had ever wanted, a perfect little cottage with roses around the door and pale blue paint peeling off of the little wooden gate at the front.

Closing the door on the rest of the world, I took a huge sigh of relief. We'd made it, we were finally installed in our new home and the children had handled the upheaval remarkably well considering. I'd shown them pictures of the ferry and the new house beforehand and it had seemed to work wonders. It wasn't usual for me to be so organised, but this was the biggest change in their little lives and I'd fully expected the last four weeks to be one long meltdown. The calm feeling of serenity lasted for all of five seconds until the arguments started above me, over who was going to have which bedroom. "Right, if you can't sort it out by yourselves, I'm going to come up there and pick your rooms for you," I threatened, as I stormed up the creaky wooden stairs. It took about half an hour and a few tears before they finally agreed that Maddy and Cassidy would share the second biggest room overlooking the little garden that rather conveniently had a TV aerial already installed. Toby wanted the room next to mine at the front of the house and I of course nabbed the master bedroom which was roughly the same size as my walk in wardrobe had been back in Bath. At least this one would be all mine and I could put as many cushions as I wanted on top of my floral bedding, without having to justify why a bed needed so many soft furnishings. Fortifying myself with a cup of coffee and feeling rather proud of my own Bear Grylls style survival skills, I soon had the beds put up and the children were playing a game of 'see who can get the bedding on the quickest,' an ingenious little idea of mine, if I do say so myself, while I started to unpack my surprisingly small amount of belongings, which didn't seem much to show for my thirty four years on the planet.

Following an impressive display of outward confidence, whilst not actually having a clue what I was doing, I finally managed to get the TV working and with their soft place to land at bedtime already sorted, I decided it was time to corral them back into the car once more to drive the short distance into Brading for some fish and chips, luckily the kids were too exhausted to even think of arguing over what they would and wouldn't eat for once. The windows of the car quickly began to steam up and the children giggled excitedly at the novelty of eating their food out of paper with the aid of tiny two pronged wooden forks. Generally I have to cook four different meals to accommodate everyone's tastes, so it was quite a relief to find something that we could all eat together. Maddy was being herself rather than Batman, which was a sure sign that she was relaxing and even Cassidy and Toby were chattering away happily in the back. The generous portions of food didn't last long and little Maddy's eyelids were beginning to droop, so we headed back to the little cottage that was already beginning to feel like home, even if there was still one room completely stacked with full cardboard boxes. I helped them get ready for bed which was thankfully and rather unusually, a drama free experience after which, Toby retreated to his enclosure with his ever present headphones firmly jammed into his ears and Maddy and Cassidy were in their room watching Frozen on DVD, for the thousandth time at least.

Once I had the kitchen sorted and everything packed away, I opened up a bottle of Merlot, pouring as much as possible into the largest wine glass I could find and opened up a pack of the kid's Quavers, because they were the nearest thing I could find to cheese and it was the closest I was likely to get to sophistication for a while. It was a novel moment, having complete command over the remote control for once. After flicking through the channels, I found the responsibility a bit overwhelming and unable to decide what to watch, I picked up my empty glass and the remains of the bottle, turned the light off and crept upstairs. It was such a relief after years of being in a couple, to know that I could go to bed and fall asleep whenever I chose, without someone tutting at me, because I was too exhausted for love making. My husband had always been ready for sex no matter what. He was always genuinely confused that if we'd had a row, or if the children had run me ragged all day, I wasn't in the mood to be romantic. For too many nights, I'd agreed to make love just to keep the peace. Don't get me wrong, it wasn't forced or against my will, but I will admit to sometimes feeling as nothing more than a vessel for his pleasure and afterwards when he went to sleep happily, I would lay there in the dark loathing him. If he ever moved the bed, he'd find nail marks embedded in the back of the headboard, where I'd tried so hard to be a good wife and not make any comments. I'd tried to talk to him about my feelings once. I'd sat him down once and explained how he always seemed to want sex even when we'd just had the mother of all arguments, whereas I needed to be in the right frame of mind, needed a little romance to get me in the mood and how that didn't mean him coming up behind me in the kitchen and grabbing me inappropriately. I just wanted to feel he cared about me and the kids, wanted him to talk to me, spend time with me, rather than his Xbox and make me laugh, he'd simply said "women," before rolling his eyes. I was so excited to be my own master for once, it had been such a long time though, that I wondered if I would ever remember how to make a decision by myself.

The thing about having children with Asperger's is that they don't tend to sleep all that well, but for once all three of my children were fast asleep before I was. Kissing Toby on the head, I pried his beloved iPad out of his hands and crept into the girls' room, turned off the TV and DVD just as the warm weather had begun to return to Arundel for the second time in one evening. Gently, I picked up the sleeping form of little Maddy in her pink Frozen pyjamas from her beanbag and put her into her little bed, lying her down next to her fluffy Olaf toy.

The bathroom in our old house had always been my one area of peace and sanctuary, another bone of contention between Michael and I. He'd always complain that I'd spent too long lying in the bath, but it wasn't as if I'd ever lay there relaxing. I'd had to shave my legs and right up to my belly button, before starting on the underarms, wash and condition my hair, put on a face mask, hair mask, apply pumice foot scrub, radiance exfoliator and luxury body wash, then once I'd dried myself, I'd had to cover myself from head to toe in intensive heel balm, hand cream, shimmer body butter and eye lifting serum, before spraying myself in my favourite Katy Perry perfume. To get ready for him, took some work and yet by the time I'd finished, he would have lost it with the kids and we'd end up rowing. Sometimes I'd wait until the kids were asleep to have a bath, so that he wouldn't have to deal with them, but then he would have fallen asleep waiting for me and wake up grumpy the next morning.

From now on, now that I was a single parent, a quick late shower would have to suffice, I couldn't leave the kids unwatched for even a few minutes. I wandered into my room, where my new bedding swallowed me whole and indulgently spreading myself out in the double bed like a starfish, just because I could, I fell into an exhausted merlot fuelled sleep all alone in my new room.

Chapter Two

Golden bands of sunlight streamed in through the heavy cream coloured curtains, hanging from an ancient wooden curtain pole in the narrow little window. As I shaded my bleary eyes from the brightness, I immediately sensed that something was wrong. I wasn't alone…

During the night, all three of the kids had somehow ended up in my bed. Maddy was cuddled up next to Cassidy, whilst Toby lay width ways across the bottom of the bed and I found myself lying on the narrow wooden frame, about to fall off the edge if I so much as sneezed. Gingerly, I placed one foot on the cool wooden floorboards and levered myself silently out of bed. Over the years, I have developed ninja worthy stealth like movement, which is somewhat of a bonus. When your children never sleep, the last thing you want to do when they actually manage to drop off, is to wake them up again.

Creeping around my little kitchen, I made myself a coffee and even boiled a couple of eggs. I desperately wanted some toast to go with them, but I couldn't take the risk of the children being woken by the aroma of toasted bread wafting through the house. On their first full day on the island, I planned to show them the sights and then tomorrow, they were due to go for a visit to their new school, a subject I'd been deliberately avoiding. So far Toby's experience of formal education and Maddy's brief spell in a pre-school hadn't filled any of us with confidence for the future. Let's face it, it's hard enough to fit into a new school at any age, but when you add in Asperger's and PDA it just makes being accepted all the more difficult and that's just by the teachers, God only knows what the other kids would make of them.

"Come on you lazy lot, we're going exploring!" My enthusiasm was answered by groans all round. "I'd love to..." Maddy began and I held my breath knowing that this really meant 'actually I hate your idea because it makes me anxious, so I'm just going to think up a random reason why I can't comply with your demand.' "But the removal men lost my shoes." Triumphant, she crossed her chubby little arms in front of her, considering the matter to be at end, now that she'd spoken. "The removal men lost your shoes?" Sometimes as a Mum trying to stop yourself from smiling is really difficult. Maddy nodded gravely "I don't think you picked a very good bunch," biting my lip, I pretended to frown. "Where they in a box then?" She shrugged her little shoulders and looked me right in the eyes, "yes," which made me worry for the future if she could lie so convincingly. I made a mental note not to trust a word that ever comes out of her cute little lips ever again. "So how did that happen when you actually wore your shoes on the journey here and I put them by the front door?"

"Ah" she said completely unperturbed and as if it was all making complete sense. "The removal men stole them when they left, I think you should ring and ask for them back."

"But I put them there AFTER they'd left." I was beginning to feel exhausted by this point and I'd only just woken up. "A thief must have come in and stolen them last night." Toby's spoon clattered into his bowl in fright and I took a deep breath, trying to decide whether to deal with my expert in Pathological Demand Avoidance or the anxious Aspie who now believed that a burglar had broken into our new house that he still didn't feel safe in yet. "Toby" I said, in as calm a voice as I could muster. "No one came in last night. The shoes are here somewhere, I'll find them."

"How do you know ?" He shot back, starting to flap his hands in panic.

"What ? I just know" I was starting to think it might be easier if we didn't actually leave the house, ever and just became hermits instead. "But what if the old owners let themselves in, they could still have keys."

"If they did" I groaned and wondered if it would be acceptable to have a glass of merlot with my toast and jam. "Then they wouldn't come in and just take your sister's shoes would they ?"

"I think you're going to have to get the locks changed just to be sure."

"Yes Toby," I knew he would keep on at me until I'd done it, so I made a mental note to find a local locksmith later. I just hoped that he wouldn't work out that the locksmith could conceivably keep a spare set and suddenly decide to let himself into our home at night, if Toby realised this then the only place he'd feel safe would be in Carisbrooke Castle. He'd already done his research on the island fortress and was satisfied that nothing could get in or out of it, after all, even Charles the First had failed to escape before being taken to London shortly after and executed and even more importantly the historic castle was just a little out of my price range. Traipsing up the stairs I located Maddy's shoes right where I'd left them under her bed. "Here you are," throwing the pair of pink sequined converse onto the floor, amazed to see that she didn't even blink, I was determined not to turn it into a battle. "Put your shoes on Maddy and we can go."

"I'd love to, but…" 'Here we go again' "my fingers don't work at the moment, sorry." I closed my eyes and pinched the bridge of my nose, the words 'don't react… don't react, she can't help it' ran around my mind in a continual loop. "Okay fine, I'll do it." She kept kicking her feet around, but gradually she realised I wasn't messing and five minutes later, I'd managed to tie the shoes securely to her feet and we were both still alive and talking to one another, which I was going to count as a win. As I stood back up, Toby kicked his trainers back off. "What's wrong now ?" How were we going to ever see the island, if we couldn't get out of the house before nightfall ? "They hurt and they feel scratchy." As I thoroughly checked his trainers, I stole a glance at Cassidy standing in the doorway with a 'what did I do to deserve this family ?' look on her face. I felt so sorry for my middle child, the other two took up so much of my time and yet she'd never complained about it. I'd have to make more time for just me and her, but my two other children might have something to say about that. "Look guys, I know you're nervous but the best way to feel settled is to go out there and have a look around the island. I've made some sandwiches and…"

"Ooh" said Maddy jumping up and down on the sofa, despite being told repeatedly that it wasn't a trampoline. "Have you made me chocolate spread sandwiches ?"

"Yes honey"

"and you haven't put any butter in have you ? I don't like butter."

"No Mads there isn't any butter in there; believe it or not, I do know what you like to eat." Happy, she ran off back up the stairs, but before I could stop her, Toby came to me with his own concerns. "I think it's a red day today." He imparted, as if most of his days weren't 'red days' which meant that Toby only wanted to eat things associated with red, it was such a regular occurrence that I actually kept red food colouring in the cupboard to be added to random foods at a moments notice. "I've packed you a red apple, jam sandwiches and a packet of ready salted crisps in a red bag, is that okay ?" He happily nodded and I congratulated myself on a rare little win, I'd actually done something right. "What about me ?" Cassidy asked, her ever present white earphones hanging around her neck. "What do you mean ?"

"What have you made for my lunch ?"

"Your favourite, ham with French mustard." I was so proud of myself for getting it right, three for three, I was on fire, surely there was a nomination for 'Mother of the Year' in the offing ? Perhaps life on the island was going to be plain sailing now we were on our own. "Muuuuum, I don't believe you, I HATE ham and mustard." And there I was, right back down in the doghouse once more, after reaching the heady heights of a happy family for all of two minutes. "Fine, I'll grab you something while we're out."

"Me too, me too" demanded Mandy who had clearly gone to her room, because she was now suddenly dressed like Darth Vader. Grabbing my hand in excitement, she pulled me towards the door "come on Mummy, you're making us late" I didn't even have the energy left to argue that I'd been the one who'd been trying to get them to leave the house for at least forty five minutes.

Chapter Three

"You do know where you're going don't you Mum?" Toby asked with all the intensity of Inspector Morse, scanning for chinks in my armour, any weaknesses in my resolve, that boy would have quite a career in CID or Special Intelligence if he wanted it. "Of course I do Toby; I have been here before you know." I turned left towards Brading and decided that if I was going in the wrong direction, I'd just keep going and tell the kids we were doing a tour of the islands landmarks. "So where are we going first ?" I felt my shoulders sag, even after nine years of being his mother I was still a rookie, I was just surprised he hadn't insisted on a printed itinerary with visuals for the day. "Well we're going to..." I wracked my brains trying to map out the island in my memory. "Sandown, where they have a lovely pier and shops and then we'll go on to Shanklin and have our picnic on the beach."
"Sounds good" said Cassidy and I was happily surprised to find that I couldn't detect even a hint of sarcasm or cynicism in her voice anywhere.
"No it doesn't" shouted Toby, "I'm not eating my food on the beach, the sand gets everywhere."
"Darth Vader can't eat" piped up Maddy "he hasn't got a mouth because of his mask." This was the worst of all outcomes, if I sided with one, then

the other ones would think I was being unfair on them, my address may as well read 'Natasha Collins, No 1 Between a Rock and a Hard Place, St Helen's, Isle of Wight.' So I did the only thing I could and said nothing.

Despite the fact that we were now into October, the sun was shining in a cloudless blue sky, just as it always had in my girlhood memories of the island. Isle of Wight Radio played in the car, not too loudly obviously and I wasn't allowed to sing along, but I silently bobbed my head in time to the music without being told off. The windows were down and despite the delayed start, it was hard not to feel as though we were on holiday, we were so lucky to be living here, it was going to be amazing, we didn't have to leave at the end of the week like all the poor tourists. "Honey are you not a little hot beneath that mask ?"

"I can't take it off, Darth Vader always keeps it on. If I took it off no one would know who I was would they ?" I couldn't think of smart replies as fast as my children, so instead I admired her attention to detail in the pursuit of authenticity and let her carry on being an evil manipulative dictator, which was a little too much like typecasting as far as she was concerned. Cassidy had a book open in her hand, but she was ignoring it, preferring instead to stare out of the window, taking in her surroundings, Toby had his knees drawn tightly up to his chest and looked every bit as though he was ready to bolt out of the car at the first set of traffic lights. "It's okay Tobes, it's going to be a fun day today, trust me." His body language hadn't changed but he didn't argue back either, so I counted that as a win. We drove through the High Street, with the children each making a mental list of the shops they planned to visit, before I turned left onto Pier Street and they saw Sandown Pier, their thoughts of anything else, instantly forgotten, even Darth Vader pushed her mask up onto the top of her tight little curls.

I pulled in at a parking space on the Esplanade, to gasps of awe when they saw the immense stretch of white sand against the calm blue waters. Whenever I'd suggested going to the beach before, I'd always been outvoted. The breeze was always too cold, the sand too grainy, too many people etc, etc. The only difference was that this time I'd not given them advance warning and they were too excited to think of their list of fears, though I knew that wouldn't last long after Toby got hit in the head by a Frisbee or some other random disaster that always seemed to befall him.

We made for the pier first and the minute we walked through the doors I realised that the lights, the wall of noise and the smell of people and foods combined, were going to create a perfect storm. Toby instantly put his hands over ears, trying to block out the sound of over a hundred arcade machines, money dropping and people talking.

"Here you go" I automatically handed him his ear defenders that represented the best twenty pounds I'd ever spent, but did mean that I could never have one of those cute little handbags I loved, because apart from the usual purse, mobile phone and set of keys I had to have room for ear defenders, hand gel for their fear of germs, pack of wet wipes, spare pairs of pants for Maddy and Toby, fiddle toys, sunglasses and a radar key for disabled toilets, which was the largest key I'd ever seen in my life, so my handbags were usually as big as Maddy herself. The banner above us, proudly announced that Sandown Pier was a 'day full of fun, under one roof.' As I'd suspected, we spent just under fifteen minutes inside, which given the noise, the aroma from several different eateries and the amount of people lurking around the two pence machines, I thought that fifteen minutes was actually quite good under the circumstances. Even though it was something of a flying visit, it had still proved long enough for the kids to con me out of thirty pounds, they work as a team, siphoning off pound coins a couple at a time, so I don't realise how much I've spent until it's too late and reminded me of a particularly clever gang of seagulls who robbed me of my food once in St Ives. As we left, Toby's face was purple and I could see that he was about to start crying. For a few seconds I toyed with the idea of pretending I hadn't noticed, but if I didn't get it out of him, I knew I'd just be storing up trouble for later. "What's up ?" My tone light, but bracing myself for a meltdown.

"I want you to go back and put more money in that claw machine. We didn't win anything." I started to think that perhaps we should have just stayed in the house and not ventured outside with the other people. "Toby, I put twenty pounds in there trying to win you a meerkat."

"But we didn't win it did we ?" he shot back. Sometimes I wondered where I got the patience to stay so calm from. "No we didn't because it's a game of chance, but maybe you should say 'thanks for trying Mummy, that was a lot of money you put in to try and win me something,' instead of moaning about what you didn't get." My words were lost on him and he grunted something non-committal, but he didn't cry or moan anymore, so maybe something got through to him after all. I was just thankful that Darth Vader hadn't been trying to get something from the claw machines as well, because if one of them had won and the other hadn't I'd never hear the end of it and they'd be fighting over the stupid toy until I took it away. We wandered down through the High Street amongst the press of tourists, but I'd spent quite enough on the pier, so I had three disgruntled kids in the back of the car as I drove to Shanklin and was seriously regretting my fun day guarantee. On any other day, I wouldn't have bothered taking them anywhere else, but Shanklin Beach is my favourite place in the whole world and I was eager to see it again. I could quite happily sit and watch the ships slowly making their way back out to sea, heading for far off destinations unknown, but I was a mum of three now and the chances of being able to sit down for long enough to see a jet ski make its way from one side of the beach to the other were completely nonexistent. Shanklin is far smaller than Sandown and the children were far less impressed than they'd been earlier. Until Toby spotted another amusement arcade and then he virtually leapt out of the car before I'd even parked. Another twenty pounds later, we left the amusements with Cassidy looking thoroughly bored, Darth Vader storming out happily as a group of children started smiling at her costume and one very happy Toby hugging some sort of plush Venus flytrap thing that he was thrilled with, but depressingly looked as though it would have

cost all of five pounds if only I could have found a shop that sold them. A few brave people, or insane I couldn't decide which, had decided to brave the unseasonable warmth and were running through the waves out into the bracing temperatures of the English Channel and for once I was deeply grateful that my three weren't big fans of the beach. "I'm hungry! You promised you'd grab me something to eat when we got here." I knew my bag had Tardis like qualities, but the kids seemed to be under the impression that my purse possessed the same abilities, however Cassidy was right, I had promised. "What would you like ?" I'd resigned myself to the fact that I was sure to be bankrupted by my own children within hours.
"Hot dog" she jumped up and down "hot dog, hot dog." Wincing, I opened my purse, hoping there was enough money in there to buy a dubious looking sausage in a roll that cost almost the same as our new little cottage. "Fine"
"I want a hot dog too." Darth Vader had presumably found a way to avoid the whole mask and not being able to eat conundrum. "I've made sandwiches for you, they're in the car."
"I don't want sandwichesssssssssssssss…." The prolonged last letter was sufficient enough to get me to crack and five minutes later I'd exchanged my soul, in return for three lukewarm flaccid looking sausages in dry finger rolls and a lemonade for them to share, I would just have to eat three warm sandwiches for my lunch.

Back in the car once more, I headed towards Ventnor, following the coastal route around the island, pointing out places I'd been as a child, we headed up through the back of the Wight, through

Alum Bay, where they made a mental note that they wanted to return when we had a day free. Cassidy was impressed by Freshwater but by the time we'd got to Cowes they were starting to get restless once again. "I think that's enough sightseeing for today, we've got plenty of time to explore. I'll head back home."

"Yippee" squealed Maddy, her curls bobbing up and down as she bounced around in her seat, as much as the seatbelt would allow at any rate and I wanted to cry with happiness at how excited she already was about our new little home. "We're going on the ferry, we're going on the ferry" she chanted. My blood ran cold and my heart missed a beat, she clearly didn't think of this as her home yet and more importantly, she'd been positively thrilled at the thought of going back to Bath. I fantasised about ramming my head several times into the steering wheel until I lost consciousness, but decided against it at the last minute, there was no point in taking it out on the car. "We're not going on the ferry honey; we're going back to our cottage in St Helen's, that's where we live now." Maddy put her hand over her eyes, in a perfect impression of me, when I've done something stupid. "Oops sorry Mummy I forgot. This is where we live now."

"That's right sweetheart." I beamed, relieved that she'd accepted the news so well, it didn't surprise me though, with PDA Syndrome, mood swings were par for the course. "We live here now, but we're going back home after our holiday aren't we ?" Oh this was bad, really bad, I thought they'd coped strangely well with our change in circumstances. "How long are we on holiday for

?" She continued, pressing me for an answer. This was clearly a sensitive subject and I had to tread carefully. Before the move I'd tried to explain that we were going to be moving to the Isle of Wight and I hadn't wanted to frighten them about the change. Scanning my memory banks I tried to remember how I'd phrased it and whether I'd given any indication that this was just a holiday. Before I had the chance to frame a sympathetic and understanding reply, Toby jumped in. "No Maddy, Mummy means this is where we're going to be living. We're not going back to Bath again, not ever." After shattering his little sister's world, Toby went back to happily playing on his iPad, completely oblivious. "But what about Daddy ?" This was so serious a question, she'd seen fit to take her Darth Vader mask off and my heart felt like it had just been ripped in two. "We'll talk about it when we get back to the cottage." I whispered, before Toby could make matters worse, luckily Cassidy was listening to music on her iPod and hadn't heard any of the exchange, it was also a comfort to know that at least Toby understood that we'd moved here permanently, so I must have done something right when I'd broken the news.

Turning the radio up louder, so that no one would feel the need to talk, I drove dejectedly back to St Helen's and our little home on Upper Green Road. We made it back with twenty minutes to spare before my supermarket delivery that I'd somehow forgotten all about, arrived. I'd been so thankful when I'd found out that my favourite store wasn't too far from the house and that they delivered. I felt a bit guilty making them drive less than five minutes to deliver the shopping, but I'd tried to do the weekly shop with three children and it wasn't easy. Maddy kept running off, thinking it was the perfect place to play hide and seek and making me age ten years every time I turned around and she wasn't there. Then there was Toby who didn't like the lights, the noise or the smell and all three of them begging for toys or ridiculously overpriced magazines offering cheap plastic inducements in little plastic bags attached to their fronts and would no doubt end up in the bin later in the week, at least when I had my shopping delivered now it cost at least twenty pounds less and I didn't feel like I needed a stiff brandy and a lie down afterwards.

   I cooked sausages and mash for tea, no peas for Maddy and no gravy for Toby, but even though I'd thought I was hungry, I ended up chasing my food around the plate instead. My appetite had flat lined when the words 'what about Daddy ?' were uttered and no amount of CPR would revive it. Bath time was the usual battle, I'd been naïve enough to believe that moving might change their hatred of being clean. I finally lured Maddy in, by saying "if you have a bath, you can either watch a DVD with Cassidy or you can have half an hour on your tablet it's up to you." My clever little daughter climbed smugly into the bath, satisfied that control had been handed firmly over to her and she splashed quite happily for ten minutes, even allowing me to wash the gravy off of her and shampoo her hair. Once Maddy was clean and dry, Cassidy had her bath and last but not least was Toby's turn. Trying to get him in the tub, was a lot like trying to get a cat in a box, but after a lot of tears and begging, mostly from me! I managed to finally get him in.

Two gigantic glasses of Merlot later and we were all in our onesies, tucked up in bed. Michael had always refused to let me wear a onesie before, he said it took away the romance and if I got one, I may as well stop dying my hair or waxing. When I'd made the decision to finally leave him, I went straight out and purchased myself a onesie that made me look rather fetchingly like a monkey. Staring out of the window, I could see Bembridge Windmill as a darkened silhouette in the distance and the monument atop Culver Down, my last bedroom had a view of the house in the street behind and cost three times more than this one. I'd truly found my paradise, it was just a shame that the children didn't particularly feel the same way… yet. Taking in a deep, steadying breath, I turned to the three expectant faces, gazing at me from the comfort of my bed, the bed I'd foolishly been so excited at the prospect of sleeping alone in. Maddy wore a Dalmatian onesie, Cassidy wore one adorned with bunnies and ponies and Toby had decided that he was far too old now for such boyish things and had opted for a navy blue fairisle design. "I just wanted to talk to you before you go to bed, Tobes and Cass you probably know all this, but I wanted you all to be together, then you all have the same information." They were uncharacteristically quiet, so I ploughed on while I had a rare advantage. "This lovely little cottage is our home now, we're not going to be moving back to Bath and tomorrow you're going to have a look

around your new school and pre-school, which you'll be starting at the end of half-term."
"What!!!!!" leaping out of bed as though it were on fire, they all started talking over one another. "Stop!" I didn't like to raise my voice if I could help it, but otherwise I'd never be heard and their school wasn't uppermost on my list of priorities right now, that was a nightmare reserved for another day. "We will talk about school tomorrow. Maddy in answer to your question earlier, I'm sure at some point Dad will come for a visit or you'll go and visit him" I genuinely had to prevent myself from shuddering at the very thought of the children leaving the island. "We haven't worked out the details yet, is there anything else you want to ask ?" Maddy bit her lip, Cassidy stared at me unblinkingly but Toby's hand shot straight up in the air. "Yes Tobes ?" I asked, nervous at what he was going to throw at me. Toby was the deepest thinker out of all three of my kids and always surprised me with his skills of perceptive questioning. "Can I go back in my room and play on my iPad now ?" Well at least I knew what was at the top of his list of priorities. "Yes Toby" grinning at my surprising little boy "you can go, thank you for giving me your attention."
"I'm going to watch a DVD then if he's allowed to leave," Cassidy swept out of the room as imperiously as anyone wearing a onesie can.
"What about you Mads ? Where do you want to sleep tonight ?" Turning on the TV, I drew the curtains and jumped into my still beautifully clean, fart free bedding. "I wanna stay here with you Mummy." As I cuddled her in, I hoped that she wasn't just talking about where she wanted to

sleep. "I do still miss Daddy though" she whispered, making my heart break for the second time in one day. "I know you do honey, I know and I'm sure Daddy misses you too, but we will be happy here, I promise." Cuddling my little Dalmatian into my side, I started to watch Emmerdale and by the time I looked back down at her, she was fast asleep with her tiny little thumb clamped in her little rosebud lips. Feeling like a fish out of water and in desperate need of a little company, I decided to keep her in my bed for the night and as strong as I thought I was, I sobbed my way through the whole of Coronation Street and it wasn't even a particularly sad episode. Had I done the right thing, moving my children to an island that until yesterday had only lived on for me in my memories ? One thing that was for certain was the knowledge that things were only going to get harder, I still had a divorce to get through and everyone knew that even the most amicable of splits always got nasty when things become official. Would the island seem so much fun when we were in the depths of winter ? Worse than all of these things combined would be the children starting school and me starting my new job all on the same day, in the same place ?

Turning the TV off, I cuddled into Maddy and promptly fell into a light restless, sleep, plagued by unsettling nightmares.

Chapter Four

At this time of year, Toby in particular was infinitely glad that I ordered the grocery shopping online. Increasingly each year, the first aisle in the supermarkets are always totally swamped with Halloween paraphernalia and it terrifies my little boy to his very soul. He sees Halloween as a hideous trial that he's forced to endure, before we can all get to the exciting Christmas goodies. So, in the interests of avoiding a trip to CAMHS the Child and Adolescent Mental Health Services and enduring months of nightmares, we drove through some quiet little back roads and past the steam railway at Havenstreet en route to a little farm shop, where they had a veritable mountain of giant pumpkins stacked up outside the door. I'd just managed to get the handbrake on before all three children attempted to catapult themselves out of the car, like clowns out of a cannon. "Wait a minute" I yelled, but as usual, mob mentality ruled the day and no one listened to the constantly nagging, poor beleaguered mother. I'd thought that the reason for this display of universal excitement was the huge array of pumpkins, but as usual with my children, I was wrong. They'd spotted the fact that there were calves in their stalls inside an open barn, next to a tiny café and opposite the shop itself. The large brown eyes and the funny mooing

sounds of four calves, reduced them all into fits of giggles. It took ten minutes of coaxing before I could get their focus back onto the important job of finding a pumpkin and reluctantly, they made their way over to where I stood, looking at a gigantic one in particular that was at least three times the size of my head. "I want you to choose a pumpkin."
"Yes, yes, yes" Maddy jumped happily up and down. It was odd, but she was dressed as a four year old girl today, because ever the contrary child, Halloween was the one day of the year when she refused to dress up in a costume. "We get to pick one each, woohoo!"
"I didn't mean that, I meant one between you."
"What ?"
"That's just rubbish."
"There's no point Mummy. We all want to do different designs, why didn't you tell us this before we left the house ?" I knew that if he were here with me, by this point Michael would refuse to buy more than one pumpkin and the rest of the day would be spent with the kids in tears and us not speaking to one another. It was the thought of how adamant he would be, that eventually made me give in, in pure defiance, so I nodded my head, unleashing another spate of jumping and cheering. "Go on then, choose one each." My euphoria at finally being allowed to make my own decisions, (once I'd had them okayed by the children first of course,) only lasted for a couple of minutes, until precisely the time when the friendly lady behind the counter with the wide smile, told me how much the pumpkins were. As I helped the kids

carrying them back to the car, I made a mental note to order them from the supermarket next year.

The kids don't do trick or treat, mainly because they get frightened of other people in scary costumes, but also because I think it's rude and a really horrible thing to do, it's basically extracting sweets and money with menace. On any other day, if a child knocked on your door at night, in a mask to conceal their identity and demanded that you give them sweets or else they'd egg your house, you'd call the police wouldn't you ? The one tradition we do have though, is to carve our pumpkins and take them up to bed, then eat sweets while watching Casper The Friendly Ghost on DVD. Michael usually stayed downstairs watching one of the many sports channels, declaring that he didn't want to watch 'that bloody movie yet again,' so thankfully the kids didn't miss his presence, Christmas however might be a different matter.

I wriggled down contentedly into the bed, as the blustery wind lashed the rain noisily against the windows outside. I'd even put the heating on low, Autumn had finally arrived on the island and the weather had changed, I was so relieved that the children weren't out trick or treating. There were three beakers of ribena, sugar free obviously, on the side table and a large glass of merlot on my bedside table, along with a big bowl of fizzy sweets on their side and a large bar of fruit and nut on mine. I looked at the kids, who were watching the film as if they'd never seen it before and smiled. Somewhere out there, other women were attending dinner parties and talking about the latest book they'd just read, others were clubbing and making drink fuelled decisions on who to date, whilst others went to the cinema to see an actual full priced film, not the cheap Kids AM animated specials and ate the extortionately priced popcorn served at the cinema with the huge buckets of fizzy drinks, instead of smuggling in supermarket bagged popcorn and cartons of juice to save money. A fair few of the mums at their old school got to lie in bed and read or watch Fifty Shades of Bondage or whatever it was called, but if I had to choose, I'd much rather be in my own bed, watching a cheesy nineties movie with my kids in our onesies, which was just as well, considering.

Once they were all fast asleep, I carefully blew out the candles, making the room smell oddly like birthday cake, crossed with a mouldy root vegetables that made me hungry and nauseous at the same time. I couldn't remember the last time that one task had kept them all quiet for the whole of an afternoon, but they'd been so involved in the disgusting job of carving out the pumpkin, with all its stringy, seed infested innards and to their credit they'd made a good job of carving out their designs. Maddy had needed a little help, but her pumpkin leered at me out of two triangular eyes and a scarily grinning mouth. Cassidy, had carved the silhouette of a witch astride a broomstick and a crescent moon, which was actually rather impressive and Toby, who thought that Halloween was just far too scary, carved his to look like Pacman chasing some ghosts. The sad thing was that although the pumpkin was a triumph, Toby had burst into tears several times whilst trying to carve it. He can never live up to his own high expectations and even though I assured him it was terrific, he still wasn't entirely happy with it. When he was like that, my heart always went out to him, its hard to imagine how even the most fun of activities can be challenging, but thanks to my own mother, I could fully appreciate what it was like to never feel good enough. The many specialists I'd seen in my time, liked to impress on me that children with Asperger's Syndrome didn't have much imagination or creativity, but my two never ceased proving them wrong.

The next morning, the blackened gourds didn't look half so impressive as they had the night before, but I knew one boy who would be happy that it was all over for another year. However, the spectre of the new school was just one day away and that was ultimately more frightening for all of us than Halloween.

Chapter Five

"There's no need to be scared, it's just your first day in a new school. No one's going to expect too much of you on your first day and people will just want to make friends with you. Being different isn't always a bad thing you know, it makes you a novelty, people will be interested in getting to know you. So plaster on a smile and just go in and do your best, don't show them that you're scared."
"Mummy open the door, I need a wee." Jumping, I slid back the lock and Cassidy burst into the bathroom, knocking me out the way as she seated herself unceremoniously down like Queen Victoria on her throne, looking less than amused. "Who were you talking to ?"
"I wasn't" I lied, loading my toothbrush with paste and shoving it in my mouth so that she couldn't expect me to answer any more questions for at least two minutes. "Must have been the neighbours" I threw back over my shoulder, as I eased myself out of the room and shut the door securely behind me, before she had time to think of a response. So far, our life on the island felt like a holiday and today was the first day of reality for all of us. Maddy was starting her new pre-school and I was starting my new job as a Learning Support Assistant at Cass and Tobe's new school, it was a big day for all of us. 'Neuro-

typical' which is the polite way of saying 'normal' children would struggle with starting a new school, in a close knit island community, but for children with special needs, it was sure to be particularly difficult and as their mother, I worried. I'd drawn lots of social stories for Mads and Tobes and the school had let us go in, during the holidays so Toby and Cassidy could look around their new classrooms without the other children there, which was all well and good, but it was when those rooms were filled and an unsympathetic teacher was in charge, that the fun would really begin. I nagged them into having breakfast and hoped that they wouldn't realise that I hadn't touched a thing myself, except for three cups of strong coffee. I didn't know if it was the nerves or the caffeine that made my hands shake uncontrollably.

"Stand still and smile… Come on smile, pretend you're happy." I managed to get one shot out of four attempts, which showed them all smiling at the same time. Maddy wore a pair of leopard print leggings, with a bright pink sweatshirt and a Superman cape, after a huge bust up, where I'd flatly refused to allow her to attend Peter Pan's Pre-School dressed in full Spiderman gear, I desperately hoped the cape would disappear before we got to the door of the pre-school. Cassidy and Toby wore grey trousers and white polo shirts, beneath navy blue sweatshirts, with the school's logo emblazoned in crisp white stitching proclaiming to all, that they were now pupils of St Cuthbert's Primary School. I'd managed to shoehorn myself into a pair of navy trousers, I hadn't worn since before I'd had Toby and a cream blouse, topped off with a beige blazer. The children had all been quiet, but well behaved and calm and it felt much the same as knowing a bomb was about to explode, but not knowing exactly when it was going to happen. With the boot filled with four coats, four lunch bags, three pairs of wellington boots, three backpacks, three juice bottles, two PE bags, two empty reading book bags, one handbag and a partridge in a pear tree, we set off. First stop was Peter Pan's. I'd already spoken to Maddy's new key worker on the phone and had probably earned myself a reputation as one of 'those' mothers. The ones who think their children are more special than everyone else's and need more babying than everyone else's, even my estranged husband was of this opinion, but to be honest I didn't care, my only concern was that their first day should be as happy and stress free as possible. Maddy clung onto my hand, not wanting to let go, until Cathy her key worker came hurrying over, narrowly avoiding concussing three toddlers with her ample hips. "I'm so glad you're here," she smiled briefly at me, but her focus was all on Maddy. "You see the thing is, I can't decide whether we should sing first or have a story and I need a real Super Hero to come and help me decide." Without even saying goodbye, Maddy followed Cathy across the room without a backward glance, chattering enthusiastically about the merits of a story and whether she could see the possible books before making a firm decision. Leading my two eldest back to the car, I was enveloped in a warm sense of relief. I'd clearly underestimated Cathy. She'd obviously remembered the two most important points I'd tried to impress on her at our meeting. Number one, don't be 'insistent' be 'persistent' and the second thing was to give Maddy choices, so that she feels like she has all the power. Putting your foot down, being demanding or punishing a child with PDA, is the absolute worst thing you can do. It's also the exact opposite of children on the Autistic Spectrum you try not to give them a choice as too many options can overwhelm them, but with those with PDA limited choices are a necessity. We were lucky that Maddy had been diagnosed so young. I'd known from around the age of eighteen months that something was different with her. Although Toby had Asperger's it can present itself quite differently in girls but there were certain similarities. A lot of Maddy's issues we put down to the Asperger's, but actually the PDA had been significantly harder to deal with. It wasn't helped by the fact that there was so much controversy surrounding PDA and not all professionals would diagnose it. There are some parents out there whose children fit the criteria perfectly, but no one will listen to them. It's because it's believed that PDA Syndrome is not a stand-alone syndrome, the person diagnosed will also be somewhere on the spectrum. When Maddy was diagnosed I hadn't even heard of it, but the Speech and Language Therapist had explained it to me and now I was completely thankful. I'd even printed out some information sheets for the pre-school and they'd obviously taken note. All in all, one down, just two more left to deliver, before I was an employed person once again, I didn't know who was the most nervous.

It was a short journey round to St Cuthbert's in Brading, but it was a journey spent in silence, something I wasn't used to. "Right we're here, let's go." I eyed Toby warily, bracing myself for refusals to get out of the car, or a full on meltdown in front of his new fellow classmates and their disapproving parents, but... nothing! He calmly got out and put his coat on. To be fair, he did march off into the playground, leaving me to bring his backpack, PE Bag, wellies, juice bottle and book bag, but that was Toby for you. Cassidy was her usual reliable self and she carried all her own bags with her chestnut coloured hair swept back into an immaculate ponytail, out of all three of my kids, she was the one I never had to worry about, she was my rock. "Do you want me to wait with you honey ?" I asked, trying to juggle Toby's stuff and dropping his PE bag in the process, not before I caught Cassidy rolling her eyes at me. "I don't want you fussing, I'll be fine." Was it okay that it still hurt that she didn't need me ? Or was I supposed to be glad that she was so independent already ? I went to kiss her on the head, but she ducked out of the way, anticipating my imminent attack. "Get off Mum. Don't embarrass me." It didn't seem all that long ago that her little face used to light up when she saw me, but now I was just an embarrassment, it was a bitter pill to swallow, even worse than when I'd found my first grey hair. After discreetly checking that my middle child was standing in line outside her classroom, I walked over to Toby. The rest of his class were all lining up and Toby was at the back of the queue, flapping his hands and jumping on the spot. I know he can't help how he is and I honestly wouldn't change him for the world, but sometimes I can't help but wish he wasn't 'the weird kid,' especially on days like this, when potential friends, potential enemies, staff and parents would be scrutinising his every move and judging him before he even had a chance to open his mouth. Fortunately, before any comments could be passed, Toby's new teacher Mr James came to stand at the head of the line, he nodded at me, the anxious mother waiting at the back of the queue, trying not to flap her hands around herself. Luckily my boy isn't as standoffish as my eldest daughter, so I kissed him on the head and whispered "be good" in an unintentional imitation of ET and with an encouraging wave, ran off in the direction of the school office.

Five minutes later, a lanyard had been placed around my neck, proclaiming for all to see that I was 'Ms Collins, Learning Support Assistant' and I was left to wait nervously in reception for my new teacher to come and fetch me. All the other LSAs were probably already setting about their tasks industriously and no doubt had been for at least half an hour and I cringed at the thought of how annoyed the class teacher would be at having to leave his or her duties to come and collect and then train the newbie. I would have preferred to have met whoever it was that I would be spending every day of the next school year with, when we'd come in to show the kids their classrooms, but it hadn't happened. Trying to put a positive spin on things, I told myself that it was probably for the best that I hadn't met the 'Hun' who would be ruling me with a rod of iron, because I would have spent the rest of the time until now, panicking and talking myself out of the job, in much the same way as Toby would have done. "Mrs Collins?" A young man who looked to be a few years younger than me and good looking enough to have stepped right out of a boy band came striding around the corner, shaking my hand enthusiastically and grinning with his perfect white teeth gleaming in his soft pink lips. "Um it's Ms Collins, I mean just call me Natasha." I could feel my cheeks burning in mortification, as he looked at me with a twinkle in his eye. I may as well have just said 'I love you, take me now, oh gorgeous one.' His hair was short at the sides and trendily long on the top, glowing golden brown under the harsh fluorescent lighting. "I'm Dave Matthews, nice to meet you. Have you ever worked in a school before?" Bless him, he was trying to make small talk with the stammering tomato he'd been unexpectedly lumbered with. As we walked, I kept stealing surreptitious glances at his clothes, they were all immaculate and clearly well-made and costly, whereas my clothes were from the bargain rails of Primark, mixed with a Sainsbury's jacket I'd had since Toby was one. If Toby wanted a Ralph Lauren jumper I would have bought him one without thinking, but I couldn't justify spending money on myself. It had always been a bone of contention between Michael and I. He liked to spend Sunday afternoons cruising the designer outlets, thinking he'd bagged himself a bargain, because he spent a fortune on something from a designer he'd never heard of and I was thankful that I'd left that life behind. He probably took his new girlfriend around them now, buying her treats and stopping off for lunch in an out of the way country pub, eating their Sunday roast

carvery in front of a roaring fire, the way we used to before we had kids. Once we'd become a family, we'd started having lunch at the food court of the designer outlet, rammed into plastic seats, surrounded by other stressed out families who were paying a fortune for cold food that we shouldn't let our kids touch with a bargepole.
"...erm, have you ?"
"Sorry ?" I asked, reddening further as I realised he'd been talking to me for at least a few seconds and totally unaware I'd been marching off down the corridor with an angry look etched across my face. "I said, have you ever worked in a school before ?" "Ah, er, no" I squirmed, feeling like I was a disappointment before we'd even reached the classroom. "I'm qualified though, I was a Nursery Nurse, in a previous life."
"How are Toby and Cassidy feeling this morning ?" He asked brightly and I liked him even more. "Oh great, great" I answered, not used to being able to talk about Toby in positive terms when it came to school settings. "They were both fine this morning, but I'm sure I'll hear all about it tonight. I'm not worried about Cass, it's Toby and my little girl Maddy that will be on my mind all day. I'm going to have to resist the temptation to run down and check on him every five minutes." I laughed, but I could tell by the almost imperceptible furrowing of his eyebrows, he didn't know whether I was joking or if I was a 'helicopter parent' who couldn't leave their kids alone for five minutes. I let out a strangled high pitched laugh and hoped that he wouldn't realise the truth, that I hadn't actually been joking. "Well don't you worry about that," he announced, suddenly

opening a classroom door and standing back to let me enter first. "I'll keep you so busy you won't even have time to think about your children." Now it was my turn to try and decide if he was joking and after ten minutes I realised… he wasn't.

"Class, this is Ms Collins," as he said the words, thirty pairs of eyes all swivelled in my direction. Ms Collins sounded so official and intimidating when he said it to a group of young children and I felt unaccountably old. "She's our classroom assistant for this year and I expect you to listen to her, if she asks you to do something, then I expect you to do it. Is that clear?" Thirty pairs of eyes swivelled back to him, nodded and then turned eerily back to watch me, as though they were a miniature robot army, waiting for my command. I could so easily have got drunk on the power of it all and it was on the tip of my tongue to command them all to get up and dance, just to see if they'd actually do it, but instead I merely smiled back and squeaked out "hello." My greeting was met with silence and I could see I was being scanned for weaknesses by thirty expert manipulators, making me want to just turn around and run away, perhaps this hadn't been the best idea in the world, maybe it would be safer and easier if I stayed at home watching daytime TV. "First thing's first, we're going to do some Maths, so Ms Collins if you'd like to sit over there and help that table please." He indicated a table of tiny ne'er-do-wells by the window. "Class get out your Maths books, turn to page forty three." And so my day started and true to his word, I didn't have time to miss the kids… much. I was far too busy trying to remember thirty children's names. There were at least four girls that I was convinced must be quads because they all looked exactly alike and three boys that I think were all called Will, so I've just taken to calling them all 'sweetie' as they're all around the age of six, they let me get away with that, though I wouldn't have liked my chances of calling a fourteen year old boy sweetie without getting a mouthful back. The morning passed in a frenzied whirl of maths, handwriting and circle time, before it was thankfully time for break. Mr Matthews kept his class firmly in his thrall with a mixture of craziness, inspiration and discipline, it was a difficult balancing act but he managed it so effortlessly that I couldn't help but be impressed. One or two of the more confident girls tentatively called me Ms Collins and I don't know who blushed more, me or them, but I found that I was actually quite good as a classroom assistant.

When I'd worked as a Nursery Assistant, I'd not been a mum and I'd seen things very differently. Even though it was almost ten years ago, I could still clearly see the gunmetal grey paint peeling off the walls and the drooping posters that had been stuck in place for at least five years and had faded so much that you couldn't even hazard a guess at their original colours. The little toddlers experienced their own 'groundhog day,' over and over again. Mealtimes were always at exactly the same time, nap time happened whether they were tired or not and the songs at both the circle times, were the same every single day. I still wake up at night screaming 'heads, shoulders, knees and toes' in my sleep and shaking all over in fear. Story time was always, 'We're Going on a Bear Hunt, The Gruffalo or The Hungry Caterpillar.' The nursery always felt like being in limbo with every day the same as the last, but working in a school was much better. The day was so varied and even I learned a few facts I didn't know, though I'd tried to conceal my surprise, careful not to let the six year olds start doubting my intelligence, I had three children of my own who did just that on a daily basis.

    Mr Matthews, or Dave as only the initiated could address him, (when there were no children around to hear,) told me where to find the coffee and kettle and off I trotted to enjoy a well-earned break. I was confident and I hoped the kids were having as good a first day as I was. The school canteen was empty at this time in the morning, but the tables were already set out in readiness for lunchtime. As I walked out of the side kitchen clutching my cup of hot coffee, the little bounce in my step disappeared and I was back to being a seven year old all over again. To my horror, I could see that all the tables were empty save for one, around which five people were sat deep in conversation, leaving one seat empty and there was my dilemma. If I seated myself with them, they might think me rude, as they obviously knew one another and might be talking about confidential matters, yet if I went and sat at one of the empty tables, they might think me standoffish and ignore me in future. When I was a pupil myself, I was never one of the 'cool kids,' yet I now found myself edging my way towards a table of cool kids in adult form and I was terrified. What if I sat down and a couple of seconds later, they all stood up and left ? Or what if I sat down and they instantly stopped talking and turned to look at me

? I was just about to commit myself to take a seat and had reached no more than five steps from the empty chair, when my name rang out clearly from behind me. "Ms Collins, you're need in the office," relief washed over me in a raging torrent of thankfulness. Spinning around, I smiled brightly at a bored looking woman with red frizzy hair I'd noticed in the reception area earlier playing with her split ends. "Just coming, is this about my ID ? Do you need to see my birth certificate ?" I was conscious that the conversation at the table had now stopped and my new colleagues and potential friends were listening with interest. "No" said the bored woman, "one of your children is in trouble and the Head wants to see you as soon as possible." I prayed for the ground to open up and swallow me whole, but as no divine intervention seemed forthcoming, I calmly put my full cup of coffee onto the table and walked with my head held high, out of the canteen.

As I followed the woman who had just humiliated me in public, the enormity of the situation hit me with full force. It had only taken Toby an hour on his first day at his new school to be sent to the Head. At his last school, it wouldn't have been so bad, but this was my workplace now, I wasn't simply being judged for ten minutes around pick up time in the playground, I was going to be judged during the day as well. St Cuthbert's is a small, close-knit school and as I reached the office, everyone obviously knew why I was there and I was ushered through to the Head's office, surrounded by hushed tones and halfhearted, sympathetic smiles. The heavy door swung open and for a minute or two I was rooted to the floor in shock. I'd fully expected to see Toby waiting for me with the Head, but instead I saw the back of Cassidy, slumped in an overly large chair. "Come in Ms Collins," demanded Mrs Williams, in a no nonsense brusque tone. The last time I'd seen this terrifying lady, she'd been shaking my hand and saying, 'welcome to the school, Natasha.' Now, thanks to Cass, I'd been demoted to Ms Collins. "I've called you here to talk about Cassidy's behaviour this morning." Glaring at my daughter's bowed head, I nodded, waiting for my new boss to continue. "I'm sorry to tell you, but your daughter has been answering back, etching graffiti onto her desk with a compass and she pushed a pupil over, causing a bruised knee. I think you'll agree it's quite an achievement for her first hour in a new school." I was mortified. Cassidy was my sensible child, the one I could always rely on not to cause trouble and she'd made up for the years of being good, in spectacularly quick time. For a girl who had just carried out a litany of damage and destruction, she seemed remarkably subdued. "Normally I would send her home and temporarily exclude her for such behaviour, but as it's not just Cassidy's first day" she looked pointedly at me, "I will allow your daughter to work with an LSA in the library, until the end of the school day. She's welcome to return tomorrow, as long as we don't have a repeat of today. Is that understood ?" Much to my embarrassment, we both nodded with our heads bowed and stepped from the room, both equally in trouble.

A young girl was waiting outside and I nearly walked straight past her as she only looked slightly older than Cassidy herself and besides I was far too mortified to want to hang around the Head's Office for too long. But she suddenly launched herself into our path with a smile. "Hello Cassidy, we're going to be working in the library together, if you want to come with me, I'll show you where it is." I smiled briefly at the petite, dark haired girl who was a witness to my epic parenting fail. "I'll see you later," I threw the words at my errant daughter as if they were poisoned daggers, but I didn't know if they'd hit their mark, because she refused to look at me or acknowledge that I'd even spoken. As I stormed along the corridor back to Mr Matthews' class, I could literally feel the blood boiling in my veins. She might pretend she couldn't hear me while she was safe within the school walls, but wait until I got the little madam home, she'd definitely hear me then. I'd go so far as to say, the whole of St Helen's would hear me tonight.

Mildly peeved that I'd missed my much needed morning coffee hit, I ignored Mr Matthews' sympathetic glances and threw myself into the literacy lesson that was already underway. Before too long, the bell rang for lunch and the horde of children ran excitedly from the room, leaving silence and a distinct smell of feet and sweat in their wake. "Can I take you for dinner?" No preamble, no nothing, just straight in there, asking me out on a date. I felt my face redden in panic and I began to stutter, trying to think of the right response. I mean sure I liked him, but did I want a relationship? I wanted to focus on the kids and then there was the whole 'don't mix business with pleasure' thing and what if it didn't work out and I had to come in and face him every day ? All these thoughts swarmed in my mind, as he said "in the school canteen I mean, I'll show you the way." I managed to stammer out a "thanks" but I'm sure that my emotions had been written all over my face and we walked towards the canteen in awkward silence. As soon as we entered, the noise was like an assault on the ears and my stomach jolted as I wondered how Toby would be coping with the noisy chaos. I scanned the room, along every row of children, heads bent over their lunch, until I finally saw my son. He was seated at the packed lunch table with a young blonde haired girl and they seemed deep in conversation over a wotsit that Toby brandished aloft between them. I couldn't see Cassidy, but I was still so angry that it was probably a good thing. One of the benefits of working in a school, is that you get to jump the queue at lunchtime. I couldn't help the smug, superior feeling I got as I sashayed past a line of nine year olds, 'you are SO pathetic' my inner self hissed, but I ignored it and ordered my sweet and sour chicken and rice instead. Following Mr Matthews to the end seats of an empty table, I seated myself opposite him and tried to be as lady like as possible, eating my lunch daintily, using a fork and everything. Since having the kids, I'd got into the rather embarrassing habit of eating almost everything with a tablespoon rather than a knife and fork and I resisted the urge to cram everything in as fast as possible. Raising my eyes, I realised he was staring straight at me causing me to blush, while I swallowed down a mouthful of rice, feeling self-conscious. "Is everything okay ? I heard you got sent to Helen Williams' office."

Sighing, I put down my fork, my appetite abruptly missing in action. "Let's just say, as long as I don't think about it, it's okay, but when I get home tonight, it will be far from okay I can assure you."
"All kids act up from time to time," he offered, trying to be helpful, but managing to sound condescending and patronising at the same time.
"Not Cassidy" I shook my head wearily, "plus, it's not like she just messed up in school on her first day, she embarrassed me on the first day in my job." I hadn't realised before how perfect his hair was and how his eyes were the exact colour of amber when the sun shines through it, they were framed by long black lashes that I would have killed for.
"so ???" Damn it, I'd forgotten to listen to him again! He should be told that he was too beautiful to look at without some private fantasy time needed and therefore it made it quite impossible to both look at him and listen at the same time.
"Sorry, I was miles away," I mumbled.
"None taken!" He pretended to be annoyed, but he had a twinkle in his eye, making me laugh for the first time in days. "I'm sorry, there's a lot riding on today. I've dragged the kids away from their home, their school and their family and I just wanted everything to go well." He opened his mouth to ask another question, but a tall, I'd go so far as to say gangly and stork like woman with blonde thin hair in a short curly bob, deliberately knocked into him. "Hello you. Did you have a good half term break ?" She just butted in as if he weren't already in conversation with me. I scowled at some chicken, speared it with my fork and rammed it in my mouth before I said

something I wouldn't regret. I couldn't be making enemies on my first day, I'd have to wait at least a week before I revealed my actual personality. So instead I drank some of the tepid water in my red beaker and remembered why I'd always hated school dinners as a child. "Yes it was great thanks, we went to Scotland for a few days."
"Were there clubs involved ?" She leant into him, giggling as if this were a private joke between them, I stabbed another piece of chicken, angrily feigning disinterest. "There were several clubs involved, it wouldn't be a holiday if there weren't; would it ?" He grinned irritatingly at the rude, flirting woman, whose dry curls bobbed like Medusa's snakes every time she made her stupid hyena laugh. "Let me introduce you to Natasha Collins, she's my LSA for this year."
'Suddenly remembered I'm here then' ran through my mind, but I plastered on a fake smile and instead, said "hi." Sometimes I despise myself I really do.
"Hello I'm Carole Shepherd, I'm an LSA in the year above your class. I've not seen you around before where are you from ? Are your kids here in the school ?" My instant dislike of her, began to dissipate a little as she bombarded me with questions. Much to my annoyance, I found myself answering them as best as I could and several others that she rattled out like a human machine gun. "Mr Matthews there's a telephone call for you," interjected one of the women who worked in the office, seemingly appearing out of thin air and looking for all the world like Dobby from Harry Potter. The odd, nervous looking little creature with a red tipped nose scuttled off so quickly that

Mr Matthews was forced to leap out of his seat and follow after her. "He's great isn't he ?" Carole, nodded in the direction of the door Mr Matthews had just left through. "He's great," I confirmed "I'm really enjoying it so far."
"It's such a shame" she sighed tellingly, taking a sip from her drink.
"What is ?" I asked, mystified.
"You know" she moved her eyebrows up and down in quick succession as if that was supposed to suddenly enlighten me. "No I really don't" I assured her, starting to get a little annoyed, why was she being so coy when she clearly wanted to talk about it ? Carole leaned in, checking that no one else could overhear and lowered her voice. "He's gay." In two seconds, the smiling assassin shattered a whole mornings worth of fantasies and hopes. "I didn't know that." I choked out, trying not to seem as though I'd just lost the potential new love of my life. "Oh yeah, he's not completely out, but he's got a boyfriend called Tristan, they've just come back from their holidays."

The rest of the day passed in a whirl of music and art and children who didn't see the need to wash their hot sticky hands after they went to the toilet, but wanted to hold my hand all the same. I was still smarting from Carole's bombshell, angry at Cassidy and worried about how Maddy and Toby had been doing all day, on top of the fact that I was exhausted following my first full days work in ten years. Cassidy was brought to me at the end of the day and without a word, we marched to Toby's classroom. My little boy was calmly perched on a seat reading a book about

British Monarchs and although I'd been missing him all day, he didn't even look up when I walked through the door. "Toby." Nothing! He didn't even flinch. Clearing my throat and trying not to sound too irritated, I tried again. "Toby, time to go home lovely." I must have got through because he closed his book and walked towards us. "Have you had a good day ?" I tried to keep it light, so he wouldn't know that I'd been worrying about him for the past six hours, but Toby knew me too well to be fooled, he just didn't particularly care what I'd been up to. "Did you know that Elizabeth Woodville's brother lived in Carisbrooke Castle ?" Not only did he ignore my question, but he didn't even wait to see if I was going to answer his, he simply walked out of the door and off in the direction of the car, fully expecting us to follow him. "He's been fine" shouted his teacher, as Cassidy and I hurried to keep up with a surprisingly composed Toby. In the car, Toby chattered incessantly about various royal kings and queens and their associations to our new island home. I deliberately avoided talking to Cassidy, preferring to let her think about what she'd done and worry about what her punishment would be. I'd even taken her iPod off of her, which I could tell she wanted to object to, but didn't dare to argue, given her behaviour.

   I left them in the car right outside and ran to the pre-school door. As soon as the door swung open, my little girl was there bobbing up and down, still in her Superman cape. Enveloping my little superhero in a bone crushing hug, I swept her up, thanking Cathy for her assurances that everything had gone well and ran the five steps back to the car. I could tell that Maddy was tired because every time I asked her a question she would just roll her eyes and growl at me. In the end, I had to accept that if she'd had a bad time at pre-school, she would have immediately declared that she wasn't going back there again, so even if she didn't want to talk about it, at least she didn't hate it there either.

I know it was unhealthy, but it had been a long day and I didn't feel like cooking, so instead of turning right towards St Helens, I carried straight on. Ever the anxious one, Toby was instantly on the alert. "You're going the wrong way, why are you going the wrong way ? Where are we going ?" So much for the nice surprise!
"Toby I just thought we could have a McDonalds for tea." Toby looked pleased and seemed ready to forgive me for using my own initiative and diverting without clearing it with him first and Maddy was bouncing up and down chanting "McDonalds, McDonalds" over and over again, it was great to see them so happy after such a long day. Then I caught sight of Cassidy in the mirror and could have kicked myself. Why would I reward her behaviour with fast food ? But I couldn't change my mind because it wasn't fair on the other two, who had been good. In the end I decided to continue to McDonalds, but warningly, I declared "you can have a McDonalds Cass, but I want you to go straight to your bedroom after." I just hoped that she wouldn't put two and two together and realise I'd forgotten all about her and her need to be punished.

Later, once Maddy was uncharacteristically sound asleep before Coronation Street had even

finished (she was normally still bouncing around wired when News at Ten was still on) and Toby was happily building a castle out of his Lego bricks, I downed a very large glass of merlot and made my way into the girls' room. The grey clouds that had been hovering all day, had finally decided to lash the island with rain, but inside was a haven for teddy bears and the little room was cast in a rosy glow from a string of pink heart shaped fairy lights strung above the white bed frame. At this time of night, Cass could usually be found writing stories, colouring pictures or cheerfully doing her homework by herself singing along to one of her DVDs, but she was obviously still in a contrary mood, because I found her seated at the end of her bed with the TV off, her knees drawn up to her chest and her arms were wrapped tightly around her legs, she wasn't herself at all. I sat myself down next to her, idly picking up a large sparkly pink rabbit and hugged it for moral support. "What happened in school today ?" I began, trying to find the right words and the right tone that said, you're in trouble, but not so much trouble that you can't talk to me about whatever's troubling you. "I had to work in the library mostly." Exasperated, I looked at her closely, but couldn't detect any sarcasm, so I fought to keep my voice low, suppressing the need to scream. "I...meant...when you did those bad things in class today." She shrugged her shoulders in a non-committal way, that was so similar to Toby, it was eerie. "Don't know" she mumbled.
"You've never done anything like this before, are you unhappy about your new school ? Has someone bullied you ?"

"No!" I noticed that she hugged her legs even tighter, resting her chin on her knees, she seemed so unhappy. "Are you missing your Dad then ?" My heart pounded in my chest and I hoped against hope that she wasn't missing Michael, because if she was, then her sadness was all my fault. "No it's not that." Tears had started to trickle slowly down her face, but I knew that my stubborn girl wouldn't wipe them away, she wouldn't want to admit that she was upset. "So what is it then honey ? I know something's wrong, this isn't like you." I tried to give her a cuddle, but she instinctively pushed me away. "Mummy... Mummy where are you ?" Maddy had just woken up in my bed for the first of her several spontaneous waking moments throughout the night and Cassidy was let off the hook for the time being, but she didn't look as relieved as I suspected she would, as I scuttled off to deal with her sister.

Chapter Six

The temperature was dipping week on week and the sky was constantly laden with heavy white and grey clouds, ready to deluge us at a moments notice. The tourists had all disappeared along with the Halloween aisles in the supermarkets and the island was left to the locals and us mainland interlopers, as we dodged the showers. I had rapidly settled into life at St Cuthbert's and the days had begun to pass in a bit of a blur, there was always a class assembly or a display to create and I found that I actually enjoyed myself. The children in my class were always coming out with things that made you smile, but would probably make their parents cringe if they knew what private information their little mini spies enjoyed randomly coming out with to anyone that would listen. Mr Matthews, or Dave as I was now allowed to call him was a great teacher and I really enjoyed working with him, even though it was still upsetting that even if I was the last woman alive, he still wouldn't fancy me. I didn't want to discuss his romantic life with anyone else and Carole had mentioned that he wasn't fully out, so I kept it to myself. Sometimes, every now and again I'd catch him looking at me and lamented that I wasn't a man.

Cassidy was still acting strange, but at least she hadn't been expelled. Maddy was doing well at pre-school, but her key worker told me that she seemed to get anxious whenever the noise levels crept up and at playtimes, they could see that she wants to play with the other children, but doesn't really know how. Toby was often having run ins with a couple of boys in his class who seemed to enjoy ganging up on him, I'd made his teacher aware of it and things were starting to get a little better, but all in all it was going quite well... inside the classroom. At playtimes I would often see him walking around, talking to himself and as a mother I found it completely heartbreaking. It was one thing to know that he didn't have friends to play with, but it was quite another to actually witness it first-hand. At night, I often gave him an easier time than I used to, because I finally appreciated just how hard his life is on a day to day basis.

Wrapping my arms tightly around me to keep warm in my winter coat, I stamped my feet in my new boots that were adorable on the shop shelf but were now killing my poor little innocent feet like a pair of soft leather psychopaths. I was in the playground waiting for Cassidy and Toby to be led off into their classrooms for another day, when over the racket I heard Tiffany's 'I think we're alone now,' from somewhere inside my handbag. I fished out my phone and accidentally answered the call, without looking at the caller first, I put it to my ear. "Hello," I hoped it wasn't one of those PPI companies, I wasn't able to swear in the playground and the temptation would be too much. I could hear someone on the other end, but I wasn't sure they'd heard me over the din of two hundred and ten excited children, trying to run off their energy before being forced to keep still for hours on end. "Hello" a little louder this time, trying to be heard. "Hi Tash, it's me." It's funny how you're whole body can shut down instantaneously even before your brain has fully processed the information. As soon as I heard his voice my mouth went dry and I honestly thought I was going to be sick onto the head of an unsuspecting seven year old, who happened to be walking past. I hadn't heard from him since we'd moved and to hear that voice so unexpectedly on the end of the line, made it feel as though he were stood right behind me, whispering in my ear. My safe little haven had been infected by him and I nearly dropped the phone, as I tried to stop my fingers from shaking. "Michael" I tried to sound calm, I didn't want to give him the satisfaction of knowing just how much he made my skin crawl. "How're the kids ?"

"Fine." I didn't really want to say anymore, but I wanted to hurt him, to let him know we were doing well without him. "They're great, they're really enjoying it here." I'd spent so long thinking of him as the bad guy, that what happened next completely caught me off guard. He started crying! "I miss you all" he sobbed as I looked around desperately for someone to help, but there was no one. Toby turned around and waved to me and Cassidy had already followed her teacher without a backward glance. I needed to get to work, but how could I leave things like this, trust Michael to decide to have a breakdown at the most inconvenient of times. "Look, I'm sorry but I have to go." I heard him sniff several times down the line and then he was all full of apologies. "I'm sorry... really sorry.... I didn't mean to.... Look can I call you later?" My whole body was screaming 'Nooooo!' But my problem is I've always been too polite and too willing to take on other people's pain, so I muttered "of course" and hung up on him.

The day passed in a whirl of imagined conversations, each of them ending in me telling Michael not to call again, if only the actual phone call had gone that way. "Up to anything nice this weekend?" Dave asked, breaking into my thoughts over lunch. Carole was attending a First Aid training course and the peace and quiet was a welcome addition, lunchtimes were normally spent with her hogging all of Dave's attention whilst simultaneously rubbishing the character of every pupil or member of staff in sight. "Er I don't know really, it's been pretty full on this week, I think the kids are looking forward to just relaxing while they've got the chance. What about you?" I tried to deflect just how boring my life really was.

All day, I carried around the threat of Michael calling me later and it left me feeling subdued and uneasy. He was the children's father, I couldn't stop him from seeing them and I had never rubbished him in front of them, but I'd moved all this way, just to get away from him. He'd made the children and me so unhappy, I just wished he could have let us go and forget all about us. To make matter's worse I had Toby's Disability Living Allowance application form to fill in, which had more pages than 'War and Peace' and with my three, getting the time to fill it in, could

genuinely be classed as 'me time.' I knew full well the minute I picked it up, Maddy would suddenly declare that she needed the toilet or Toby would have a meltdown over a computer game that he couldn't work out. Walking back to my classroom, I happened to pass Mr James, Toby's teacher. I smiled in acknowledgement and made to walk by, when he put out his hand to stop me. "I was hoping I'd bump into you." He began, politely. "What's he done ?" I preferred cutting to the chase, but Mr James began to blush pink underneath his brown close clipped beard. "Nothing, nothing, it's just the flapping. Does he do that a lot at home ?" I had to think for a couple of minutes, Toby had so many funny little quirks that I'd almost stopped noticing them. "He usually only does it when he's stressed out about something. Is he doing it at particular times of the day ?"
"No" he shook his head, "he does it at any time and it can be quite distracting for the other children." I took a deep breath before answering, this was starting to sound as if he was blaming Toby for doing something he couldn't help and I momentarily had déjà vu, I'd been here before with his Bath school. "Have you talked to Toby about it ?"
"Not yet" he admitted, blushing even more. "Now that I know it's an anxiety thing, I'll have a quiet word and see if there's anything I can do to make things easier for him and try to avoid raising his tension levels. This morning, he's had a camera and has been taking photos for his visual timetable, he's enjoyed being in charge."

"Thank you" I smiled tightly and hurried off to the safety of my classroom, every day was a reminder of how hard things were for Toby and so much of that depended on how understanding the adults around him were, lucking Mr James seemed to have the measure of my son. 'Have a word with Toby about flapping' was mentally added to my list of 'to do' items that seemed to never get done, no matter how hard I tried. Every morning, Maddy and Toby were forever trying to convince me that they should stay home from school, but once I'd managed to cajole, tease or downright bribe them to go in, they were usually fine, but I could never lower my guard for too long, something always surfaced, sooner or later and by working as an LSA I'd made it even easier for the staff to stop me and talk about my children's shortcomings.

The day passed in a whirlwind of bug hunting around the school lake and sticking thirty mosaics together for their project on the Romans and all too soon I had three tired children bundled into the back of the car, heading for home. The nights were really beginning to draw in, making the cottage seem even more homely than usual. In the middle of the day, I often found myself fantasising about getting everyone home and after tea, sitting around the roaring fire in our onesies, chatting about our day, until it was time for me to load the dishwasher and watch my soaps, whilst the kids returned to their tablets and iPods in their rooms, which fortunately, was how our nights normally went. Normally...

"So what's for tea ?" Toby asked, pulling open the fridge with one hand and the freezer with the other, before closing them and then staring blankly

at the kitchen cupboard for several minutes, before declaring that there was nothing to eat. "What do you want to eat Tobes ?" Trying to remain calm and positive was a daily challenge.
"What's the point in saying ? We probably haven't got it anyway." He crossed his arms defensively over his body and I took several deep breaths, before my head exploded. "Why don't you tell me anyway ? Then if I don't have it, perhaps I could get it for you for tomorrow's tea ?" I was forced to wait, while he considered my words and then scanned them for a) sense and b) weakness in my logic. Deciding that answering me was a win-win situation for him, he chose to favour me with an answer on this occasion. "I'd like some of those little barbecue chicken pieces you get, you know the ones that look red ?" I knew where this was going "and then can you do me some potato wedges, but cover them in red food colour stuff first and then some red kidney beans ?" Luckily, this was his favourite meal and knowing him as well as I do, I always have reserves in the freezer and the cupboard as back up. "No problem mate, I'll get right on it." With his red food ordered, he marched off happily in the direction of the TV.
"Maddy!" No answer.
"Maddy!" Still no answer and I was starting to lose my calm, fragile demeanour. "Maddy!" Louder this time,
"what is it ?"
"come here please"
"why ?"
"Because I'm your mother and I asked you to, now come here!" I was starting to get a headache.

"Yes Mummy?" It was truly unbelievable, how she could pull off such a picture of innocence when required, just when you were starting to get cross with her. "What would you like for tea ?"
"Nothing, I'm not hungry." Believing the conversation to be at an end, she turned on her heel and made to return to the living room. "You need to have something to eat."
"No!" I'd done it now. I'd made her put her foot down, thus triggering the PDA and tiptoeing on the point of no return, I tried a different strategy. "That's okay honey, I just thought that you might want to choose something for your tea, but you're only little I doubt if you could do it anyway, perhaps when you're a big girl like Cassidy..."
"I am a big girl." Mission accomplished, she was really furious now.
"I'm not sure," I replied, pretending to mull it over.
"Yes I am, I want fish fingers and waffles please." She skipped off into the living room, while I rooted through the freezer, with a wide self-satisfied grin.

 I'd just managed to put Maddy's tea in the oven, when my mobile rang, vibrating perilously close to the edge of the kitchen worktop. I'd been worrying about it all day, yet when I saw 'Michael's Phone' on my screen, it was still a shock to the system and I was filled with the desire to throw the phone in the freezer and run away, but I knew he'd just keep ringing if I ignored him, so deciding it was probably best to get it over with (kind of like ripping off a plaster,) I reluctantly answered.
"Hello"

"Hi Tash it's me again," there was silence on the line, and I couldn't stop myself from loathing him for stating the obvious as he hesitated, expecting me to answer. "What do you want Michael ?" I asked, sensing three pairs of large flapping ears suddenly twitching in the other room. "Oh!" he exclaimed, shocked at my abruptness, which seemed a bit pathetic given that I'd left him and moved to an island to get away from him, I was hardly going to be friending him on Facebook any time soon. "I was just wondering how the kids are ?" A block of ice, settled in my stomach. "They're fine, I told you that this morning when you rang." "Come on Tash" he said in that patronising tone that I hated, yet knew so well. "I'm trying here." "Trying what ?" Emotions were surfacing that I hadn't felt in months and I hated him for it. "Trying to be nice, I miss you all." His voice broke and I softened a little, despite myself. "They're doing well, they're settling into their new school and pre-school."

"Do they ever ask for me ?" His voice was so full of hope that if I told him the truth, it would be like kicking a puppy in the face, but I didn't want to lie to him either or give him any false hope. "They haven't asked outright, but it was hard for them at the start, Maddy misses you and she couldn't understand why we weren't going home at first." "Neither could I." Resisting the urge to slam the phone down, I paced up and down the kitchen checking the kid's teas weren't burning and trying hard not to be too argumentative, but it was hard to see him as vulnerable when I'd spent years of seeing him as a bully. "I'm coming over to the island, I need to see you all." My heart sank. If I said no, I was actively keeping their father away from the kids, but if I agreed, I was also accepting this huge negative influence back into their lives. This was our new life, one I'd fought for and planned for months so to see him here, on my island built of happy memories and fresh starts was soul suckingly depressing, like a cloud passing over the sun. I closed my eyes, trying to keep the cursing in, "fine."

"That's great," he sounded so relieved "I've been told I can have some time off work, so I'll book the ferry and somewhere to stay and I'll let you know when I'm coming." What had I unleashed ? What was I going to tell the children ? Would this destroy the progress we'd made so far ? Was he purely only coming to see the children ? Would he try and persuade me to return to Bath ? All these thoughts passed in a split second, "fine" was all I could reply and ended the call. I'd just peered in the oven, when Cassidy ventured into the kitchen. I smiled warily, wondering how much she'd overheard. "If you've finished cooking Maddy and Toby's tea and talking on the phone, I wondered if you wanted to know what I wanted for my tea." Cassidy always had the knack of making me feel like the worst mother in the world, I swear it's a God given gift. "I'm sorry Cass I dealt with theirs first and then my phone rang. I haven't cooked anything for me yet either, what would you like ?" I didn't realise seven year old girls could paralyse you with a withering glass, but Cassy had really nailed it. "Anything, you know me, I'm never a problem, I never make any demands do I ?" She turned on her heel, like a miniature Scarlet O'Hara and swept dramatically from the room without

another word. "I'm really going to have to speak to that child," I muttered, shaking my head in consternation and carried on dishing up the tea for Toby and Maddy. Once they were happily tucking into their food, I popped two pizzas into the oven for Cass and I. Fortunately, I remembered the pizzas before they were totally burnt and after tea we managed to get a little homework done, bath time was the usual nightmare, but we got through it and I managed to finally get them in my bed in their onesies, all looking expectantly at me. I cleared my throat, not really knowing where to begin. "I had a call from your Dad today." I held my breath, but they didn't react, so I carried on, "he said he wants to come over and visit."
"Is that it ?" Toby asked, relieved I nodded, perhaps it wasn't such a big deal to them after all. "I'm going to my room then." Tobes announced and skulked off to his own little sanctuary. "I don't want to see Daddy" Maddy screamed and pulled the pillow over her head "he shouts all the time." More worrying though was Cassidy's reaction, she didn't even move, she just sat there staring at me, unblinkingly. I wanted to agree with them, tell them that I wouldn't answer the door when he got here, but I'd watched enough Jeremy Kyle to know that I had to be the bigger person and encourage them to have a healthy relationship with their father, even though he'd done nothing but yell at them and exacerbate their Asperger's at every opportunity. If he was doing it on purpose then there was some hope that he could change, but he genuinely didn't even realise he was doing it and that was the saddest thing of all. The second that he got annoyed, he raised his voice Maddy

would be left grimacing with her hands clamped over her ears, begging for him to stop, but he'd still carry on. It got so bad that I couldn't even go for a bath towards the end. As soon as I'd lower myself into the warm bath water, I'd hear raised voices and Toby would storm upstairs in tears. Once I even had to get out, covered in soap suds and go downstairs to referee, which was always like dealing with four kids, instead of three children and one adult. Michael would say to me in a perfectly calm and reasonable manner, "all I said to him was, no you can't have a ham sandwich at the moment and he flipped." Every time, I would say "that's how you think you said it Michael and that might be how it sounded in your head, but when you said it to Toby it was abrupt and aggressive and your voice was far too loud, plus what's wrong with him wanting a ham sandwich ? He never eats, so if he asks for something, then why not do it ?" This was always how the arguing began. Michael thought I was mollycoddling Toby and I thought he was unnecessarily unhelpful and far too strict. I really didn't see how a few weeks apart were going to change that. I just had to hope that he'd come over for a flying visit and then disappear back to Bath and leave us all alone. How could I let him take them back for a home visit ? How could I bear to think of Maddy and Toby lying there in the dark with a man who actively ignored their Asperger's and PDA ? I began to hyperventilate, so I grabbed a medicinal, fully guaranteed nerve calmer, large glass of merlot and by large glass, I meant one of those huge glasses that could also be used as a vase and can comfortably accommodate a full bottle of wine. I couldn't do anything to prevent the inevitable, so I distracted myself by filling out the Disability Living Allowance renewal form, another reason for drinking myself into an alcoholic stupor. On my online Facebook group for parents and carers of children with Autism, I often read messages from people who dreaded filling out the epic novel and I must admit if your child has other very definite disabilities, then the form might be a little easier to fill in, but with children on the spectrum, nothing's as black and white as the form would want you to believe. General advice always seems to be that you should base your answers on your child's worst day, but it still means that a lot of parents and carers who really need the financial assistance, don't like to apply because they feel that they don't deserve the help, because each day is totally different. Personally, I didn't have a problem with filling it in, my problem was with the waiting, it often took up to eight weeks to get a reply and patience has never been a virtue of mine. Three quarters of a glass of wine later and the form was complete. It was never a nice thing to have to sit and put all of Toby's negative points and insecurities down in pen, but it was for Toby's benefit and that's what I had to keep reminding myself, though I still felt like a huge drunk queen of betrayal.

 I awoke at four in the morning with a start. I'd dreamt that Michael had kidnapped me and I was trapped in the boot of his car onboard the Isle of Wight ferry, while the unsuspecting kids happily sang carols on the backseat. Swallowing my panic, I let my heart rate lower and looked around me. All three children were in my bed, all sound asleep for once, so I snuggled back down, happy that they were with me and we were all safe, but annoyed that I'd woken myself up when I had children who did that for me on a daily basis. Not knowing how long it would be, before the next one woke up, I forced myself back to go back to sleep and thankfully I didn't have any more nightmares, well for one night at least.

Chapter Seven

"Why is Cassidy up so early ?" Toby was instantly suspicious of any differentiation in the day to day routine and Cassidy already seated at the table eating her breakfast before him had completely thrown Toby. "She's got a dentist appointment," I carefully kept my back to him, deliberately unloading the dishwasher so I didn't have to look him in the eyes. "You haven't written any appointments on the calendar for today." He came to stand in front of me, knowing that I was trying to avoid him and that something wasn't quite right. "She had a bit of toothache yesterday, so I'm taking her for an emergency appointment, okay ?" He scanned for lies but couldn't detect any, which meant I was getting a lot better at telling him fibs, thankfully Cassidy hadn't said a word. "What's going to happen to me and Maddy then ? Who's going to take us to school ?" I was glad I'd had my morning coffee, before this interrogation. "I'm going to be taking you and Maddy as usual, it's just that instead of going in to Mr Matthews' class straight away, I'll be taking Cassidy for a quick visit to the dentist." He seemed to relax when he knew his own routine wasn't going to be affected and went to sit with Maddy on the sofa, playing on his iPad as she watched her morning kids' programmes. I winked at Cassidy who smiled back at me knowingly.

Once Maddy had been safely deposited at pre-school dressed as a policeman, we waited until Toby disappeared into his classroom and walked back towards the car in silence. "So where are we really going ?" Cassidy asked as soon as we were safely in the car, out of earshot of everyone. "We can't go too far, we've only got about an hour or so. That should be enough time to get to Shanklin." I couldn't tell if she was disappointed at that or not. "Why Shanklin ?" She might not have a diagnosis like her brother and sister, but she was just as adept as them at asking direct questions which weren't always that easy to answer. "As a kid, I always went to Shanklin with my parents and we always had fun, it's special to me because it reminds me of my father at his happiest, before we lost him." My eyes misted up with tears making it hard to see the road ahead and the lump in my throat was almost impossible to swallow down. "I wanted to talk to you and that was the first place I thought of." I couldn't tell if my news had gone down well or not, but she didn't argue at least. The roads were relatively clear and we sailed through Lake and on into Shanklin in good time. We listened to the radio as we went and made small talk about something funny that Maddy had said or how angry Toby had got when he found out that I'd accidentally dropped the small bottle of red food colouring on the floor. I think she knew deep down what I wanted to talk to her about but she was putting the moment off for as long as she could, she'd obviously been taking notes from her little sister on deflection and avoidance. I just hoped that she wouldn't actually have any dental problems in the near future or I might have some explaining to do.

Pulling into a parking space in the old village, I led her to a tea shop that my dad used to take me to when I was Cass' age. The little bell sounded as I opened the door and I swear it hadn't changed in decades. We sat at the table reading through the little leather look covered menu, it took Cassidy ages to decide what she was having, because she kept getting distracted by looking around at the other customers and the waitresses in their spotless aprons. "What are you giggling for ?" I don't think I'd seen her so happy in ages. "Maddy and Toby would love it here, but they're in school."
"Shall we come again, with them ?" I was surprised at how much she liked the nostalgic little tea rooms. "No, this is our secret place." My other two were such a handful twenty four hours a day that I'd forgotten about my quiet, invisible, middle child. I was such a cliché mother. "I'm sorry," I watched her as she made short work of her chocolate sundae. "Is it because you feel like you're not getting any attention from me, that you've been acting up at school ?" She nodded, but continued giving all her attention to the sundae. "I'm sorry Cass, it's been really hard over the last few months and they don't mean to, but your brother and sister take up a lot of my time and what with one thing and another, it hasn't really left much time for me to concentrate on you. You're the one who doesn't complain, you're the one I rely on to be sensible and that's wrong of me." Her large doleful blue eyes regarded me over her thick chocolate sauce moustache. I handed her

a napkin and she giggled as she saw how much mess she'd made, when she'd finished she reached across the table and put her little hand on top of mine. "It's okay Mummy" she said, with wisdom in advance of her few years. "I don't blame you and I don't blame them, but everything was changing and I missed my old school and my old friends and I got angry." I sighed and closed my eyes, rubbing the tension in the temples, I hadn't even thought about how Cassidy had felt about moving. Toby had hated his old school and I'd only seen the school move from his point of view. "Oh Cass, I am so sorry." She squeezed my hand. "Mummy you had to move, we all know that, we just want you to be happy too and I have made some new friends in my class. I'm just glad that everyone's happier now." All I'd seen was the chaos of it all, I hadn't even had time to sit down and reflect on whether we were any happier, but clearly Cassidy thought we were and that meant the world to me. "Whenever you need to talk to me about anything, let me know and we'll come here and talk over ice cream, deal ?"
"Deal" she grinned. As I finished my coffee and plain scone with lashings of strawberry jam and thick fresh cream (well it would be rude not to, we were in a tea room after all,) I found myself staring at an empty little table in the window and remembered how I'd sat there with my father. Where had the time gone ? How was I the grown up all of a sudden ? Would he have been proud of me and the kids ? My mother always thought we'd gone to the amusements, while she sat in the hotel drinking gin or shopping, but my dad would bring me here to talk about anything that was troubling

us, it was how we survived the one woman hurricane that was my mother and now it was the place my daughter and I would come to help us survive living with Toby and Cassidy. God I felt old!

I paid for our food, leaving a tip for the grey haired waitress who'd nearly spilt Cassidy's sundae over her and was straight out of a Victoria Wood sketch and bundled Cassidy back into the car under strict orders that she couldn't tell anyone where we'd been and stick to the dentist story. When I dropped her back at school, we were both more at peace than we had been in weeks.

Chapter Eight

Every day during the school term I'd had to nag, threaten and manipulate my children into getting out of bed at eight am, yet whenever there was a school holiday or a weekend, they inevitably stayed up even later at night and were always, without fail, awake at six thirty in the morning, telling me it was time to get up. I was starting to have my suspicions that they'd even devised a rota system to ensure that I was never allowed to have a lie in, I had no idea why they hated me so much. "What are we going to do today Mummy?" Maddy bounced up and down excitedly in the gloom of my bedroom. "I don't know, let me have a coffee first and I'll have a think about it, okay?" "Let's go to McDonalds," Maddy bounced even higher, in danger of falling off the bed completely. "Or we could go to the Dinosaur Museum again," Toby popped his head around the door with a hopeful expression on his face. Cassidy tried to slip in unnoticed, as usual, letting her brother and sister argue over what we should do for the day. "What do you want to do Cassy?" I asked and the other two immediately fell silent, confused at the unexpected turn in events, they were so used to deciding between themselves what we should do, they hadn't even thought about what Cassidy might like. "Well... I...err... really want to go to

Busy Bee's Garden Centre, all my friends in school have been talking about it."

"No, I'm not going to a Garden Centre, that'll be boring." Maddy declared, while Toby sat ostentatiously rolling his eyes. "Well tough luck, because that's where we're going today." It was only there for the briefest of moments, but I caught such a look of joy on Cassidy's face that I was even more determined to do what she wanted for once. Accompanied by groans and reasons why we couldn't possibly visit a garden centre, I managed to bring them to a compromise of sorts. They agreed to stop moaning, as long we went to McDonalds, once we'd finished at the garden centre. It was only a short drive to get there, which was always a bonus, the kids tended to annoy one another if they were forced into confined spaces for overly long periods. "So why did you choose the garden centre of all places ?" I asked curiously, our family weren't known to be keen gardeners. "They've got a huge Christmas display, I thought it might be fun."

"Why didn't you say that in the first place ?" Toby demanded, outraged. "Maddy and I wouldn't have argued if we'd known that."

"Maybe I just wanted to see who Mum would side with." Cassidy replied quietly, leaving Toby shaking his head, as he looked out of the window.

The garden centre was obviously a huge attraction at this time of year and I had to circle the car park several times before I managed to grab a parking space. The kids were bouncing around, eager to escape before I'd even turned the engine off, but I didn't reprimand them, it was nice to see them united in their excitement for once. The inside of the store was an assault on the senses and the sort of place that would normally send their autism related anxieties through the roof, but the involvement of Christmas seemed to neutralise all the scary stuff. Every centimetre of visible space seemed to be covered in different fairy lights, some were clear white, some were multicoloured, whilst strings of red lights chased one another around the store and every piece of wall space contained ornaments. A giant, leafy green Christmas tree proudly took centre stage and I idly wondered just how long it had taken to adorn it with so many decorations, I would have given up halfway through, it was difficult enough to decorate a six foot tree to be shoved in a corner of the living room. Everywhere you looked there were Christmas delights on offer. Colour coded decorations were in one corner, dancing musical penguins and Santas took up their own section, there was another, full of different stockings, another part was a miniature little village complete with moving train and light up cottages that would have cost a fortune to replicate at home and a darkened section that contained canvas pictures, which when switched on, lit up with tiny LED lights and as soon as you walked down one of the aisles there was even more to look at. I kept the kids close, knowing how easily they could get lost, especially when distracted by so many highly coloured temptations and slowly moved forward. It took a lot of "Mummy look at this" and "yes, but put that back and don't touch" before we finally made it all the way around the Christmas Department, ending up at the tills, next to a

gigantic snow globe. "This place is brilliant" Maddy declared, "can we come again ?"
"I don't know" I laughed, "you'll have to ask Cassidy." My eldest daughter, beamed with her newly found importance, "I'll think about it" she winked at Toby, who couldn't cope when it came to not being specific. "what does that mean ?" He asked, hopping from one foot to the other, "it means that your sister is pleased you like it here and we'll probably end up coming here again." I rubbed his shoulder, trying to calm him down. "Well she could have just said that" he muttered annoyed for all of five seconds until a singing polar bear caught his eye. At the till, Cassidy and Toby walked off to look at some adorably fluffy huskies that had been placed unhelpfully next to the door, whilst Maddy my little shadow stayed next to me. For once, she hadn't dressed in a costume and I hoped this meant that her confidence to be herself was beginning to grow. The lady in the elf hat serving us, kept up a lively chatter, commenting on the weather and the items we were purchasing, while I tried to remain polite, pack our stuff into bags and keep an eye on my two eldest. "Are these for you ?" She asked Maddy, while brandishing a plush Santa and a plush reindeer at her, making Maddy hide behind me in a panic. "Oh she's shy," she smiled and I treacherously smiled back, when inside I was screaming, 'she's not shy, she's got autism,' but I knew that she was only trying to be friendly and I didn't want to cause a scene and upset Maddy all the more, so I simply paid for the goods and left. It cost a small fortune and we had a boot full of expensive Christmas goodies as we made our way

to McDonalds, but the children had enjoyed their morning and I liked the fact that we were starting our own traditions for our first Christmas on the island. They hadn't mentioned anything about their father coming for a visit and not wanting to rock the boat, I didn't either. When we returned home, I made myself a coffee, as the kids chattered wildly about the decorations we'd bought and where they wanted to put them once we began trimming up for Christmas and I felt filled with hope for the first time since we'd moved. I turned on the TV and it was only after I'd managed to watch two whole episodes of Coronation Street's Omnibus that I started to worry. Why was I being allowed to watch what I wanted in peace ? Something was wrong. I nearly tripped due to running up the stairs so fast "are you guys okay ?" I asked as I literally fell into Cassidy's bedroom. Three pairs of curious eyes looked up at me in surprise. "We're fine, we're just choosing our Christmas presents from the Argos catalogue," Toby assured me. I nervously glanced at the lists which all looked alarmingly lengthy. "I'll be downstairs if you need me and don't forget you're just trying to give Santa an idea of what you want, you're not demanding everything you put down you know." Things were going so well, I thought I deserved a little treat, I was rummaging in the cupboard trying to find something that the kids wouldn't mind me having of theirs or at the very least, something they wouldn't miss, when my mobile started vibrating all across the kitchen worktop again. My heart sank as I saw it was Michael calling, how did he know when I was in the kitchen on my own ? I'd

privately hoped that he'd find out how much the ferry fees were and decide to forget all about his visit after all. "Hi Tash" he said before I could speak.
"Hi" I wanted to sound breezy and as though I didn't care, but annoyingly my body just shut down whenever he called and I could only communicate in words of one or two syllables.
"How're the kids ?"
"Fine" I said woodenly.
"I'm going to come over and see you all on the twenty second of next month and then I'll be coming back to Bath on Christmas Eve. Is that okay with you ?"
"Fine" I muttered, relieved that he would have gone and left us alone by Christmas Day. I would never have forgiven him if he'd ruined this, our first island Christmas. He'd always been a mixture of the Grinch and Ebenezer Scrooge rolled into one, whenever Christmas was concerned, even having his own children had never changed his outlook. I'm the sort of person who starts getting excited about Christmas in July and had always had the attitude that those people who are tired of Christmas are tired of life, looking back I should have known that we were never going to work out in the long term. "Okay, well give the kids my love and I'll see you all then."
"Will do, bye" I pressed the button ending the call and dropped the phone on the worktop as if it were a poisonous snake. "Muuuuummmmm."
Forgetting all about my estranged husband, I ran up the stairs two at a time, wondering what disaster I would be met with, but the children were all sat around the Argos book with their even

longer lists in front of them. "What's up ?" I tried not to let them see how unfit I was, after a simple run up one flight of stairs. "When can we put the Christmas decorations up ?" Gulping down some breaths and holding the stitch in my side, I didn't know whether to laugh or cry. "Maddy, you called me all the way up here to ask me that ?" She nodded solemnly, her curls bouncing along in affirmation. "It's important" she confirmed, as the others nodded their agreement. "Um, I don't know" I admitted, "I'll have to think about it. But we'll do it soon I promise."

"What after tea ?" Maddy had started to bounce again.

"No not today honey. Let me think about it." Her bottom lip was thrust out and her cheeks were starting to redden, all signals that threatened an imminent meltdown. "Why don't you carry on with your list for Santa, that's the most important thing for now. Otherwise how will the elves know what to make ?" Maddy's mood swings were often like a light switch and instantly she went back to her Christmas list, crisis thankfully averted.

Later, when the children were safely tucked up in bed and asleep, (until one of them woke up and took over the first watch,) I took advantage of the rare silence. In the light of the flickering flames, I read their Christmas lists. How different this year was going to be, compared to the last one. I was used to having Michael to discuss things with and my family to help look after the children, whilst I snuck off to buy their presents. This year, I was going to be completely on my own and to be perfectly honest the thought terrified me a little, even though it had all been my own decision. I'd just decided to call it a night and try to get as much sleep in as possible before I was rudely awaken by one of the kids, when my phone suddenly burst into life, brightening the room in its eerie glow and beeping to announce proudly that it had a message to give me. No one had ever sent me a text so late at night before and I was intrigued and even a little bit alarmed. 'Hello, we're going to be coming to see you at Christmas, love to you all, Mum x.' One minute I'd been lamenting the lack of family and now I found myself lamenting the prospect of family coming to stay. My mother had never been as accepting of the kid's diagnoses as I would have liked and as such, things had been strained between us. I tolerated her for the kid's sake and she regarded me as an over fussy, over anxious mother whose children were fine, except for their overbearing mother. She also firmly believed that 'Autism' was 'just a made up word to account for lack of parenting skills and discipline in this country.' A statement that had prevented me from talking to her for several months and no amount of discussion or literature could completely change her mind. I'd spent hours explaining to her that I didn't randomly 'thrust a label' upon my kids and regardless of whether they'd seen a paediatrician or not, their needs would still be the same and no they weren't just 'quirky.' My mother looked like Goldie Hawn and in her head, she had the benevolence of Mother Theresa, but she actually had the personality of Katie Hopkins where I was concerned. Despite my issues with her, the kids liked to see their gran and I'd decided to let it wash over me, as long as the 'washing over' was aided by gallons of merlot or malbec. Another shock was that my mother knew how to text, I was surprised that she even had a mobile phone, let alone being so advanced as to send me a message. I pressed the call button, we needed to talk. What if she was planning on being here when Michael was here ? I didn't think I could handle my parents and my soon to be ex-husband together on Christmas. "Hi Mum."

"Hello dear, you got my text then ?"

"Yes, how are you ?" I thought I'd better at least pretend to be interested in her life, before I started to interrogate her over her Christmas plans. "Fine, I went to meet Margaret in Waitrose Café today and we had a lovely natter. Her Barry's just started his new job in Plymouth as a Doctor in a hospital down there." I bit my lip and rolled my eyes, no matter how unprepared, my mother never missed a chance to belittle me, by pointing out how well her friend's children were doing at life and hinting what a disappointment I'd become to her. "Good for him." I murmured, trying to keep the bitterness out of my voice.

"Yes it is," she shot back acidly,

"anyway about Christmas." I didn't want the conversation turning into a fight; it was time to get down to the matter in hand. "John and I thought it would be nice for us to come over and see you at Christmas, I haven't been to the Isle of Wight for years and it would be wonderful to see the children again." So in a nutshell, they were only coming over for nostalgia and the kids, I didn't fit into this at all. "When were you thinking of coming over ?" I hoped she didn't notice how worried I sounded.

"Well we thought it would be nice to come over on Boxing Day for a few days." That was a relief. Michael would be leaving on Christmas Eve and they wouldn't be arriving until Boxing Day, which meant that I still had Christmas Day as sacred, alone with my children. "Where are you going to be staying ?" A lot of the hotels and B&Bs offered Christmas packages and I hoped they wouldn't be staying too close to us. "With you obviously," she sounded rather affronted at my unintended insult. "But we've only got a small cottage, there's nowhere for you to sleep," I gasped, in panic. "Don't be silly, of course there is. We'll stay in your bed and you can stay in with the children or on the sofa if that doesn't suit you. Anyway, I've got to run, John's making the gin and tonics all wrong. We'll see you all on Boxing Day." I threw my mobile onto the arm of the sofa and watched as it bounced off of the furniture and onto the floor. How was I ever going to get through this Christmas and make it special, when so many ghosts of Christmas pasts were threatening to ruin it ?

Chapter Nine

"No, Toby just wait a minute please… we have to put the lights on first… Maddy, no, put that down and wait." Trimming up the house was supposed to be a magical memory for my children to hold onto into adulthood and yet all I'd done so far, was to shout at them to stop and my blood pressure had risen quite significantly over the course of the morning. Because they were kids, they just wanted to throw everything and I literally mean throw everything at the tree, hoping some of it stuck and I was currently the bad guy for pointing out that there was an order to these things.

We'd put one of the music channels on the TV to keep us motivated with Christmas classics and I don't like to appear paranoid but instead of the usual fun Slade and Shakin Stevens songs, I'd been subjected to 'All I want for Christmas is you,' 'Please come home for Christmas,' 'It'll be lonely this Christmas,' 'Blue Christmas,' followed by 'Last Christmas.' It was a good thing the kids were here or I'd be under a blanket crying on the sofa. I'd even made hot chocolate with mini marshmallows and homemade donuts covered in icing sugar, trying to get the kids in the festive mood. The living room floor was completely covered with boxes and it looked just like when we'd first moved in. "Be careful" I admonished

over and over again, as they pulled out various treasures wrapped in yellowing newspaper, most of which I'd forgotten we had. "Oh look there's our stockings" exclaimed Maddy, pulling four crumpled red velvet stocking out of the box before I could stop her. "Are you going to hang Daddy's up here too ?" I inwardly cursed myself for not thinking to check the boxes of memories, before letting the kids loose on them. "No sweetheart, but we can give it to him to take back home can't we ?" Throwing the offending stocking back into the box, Maddy carried on searching for forgotten decorations and seemed to cope with the fleeting disappointment well, though I'd wanted to weep for her hopeful little face, when she'd talked of her dad. Cassidy pulled out my prized collection of nutcrackers. "Cool" said Toby, who'd always loved them too.
"I think they're ugly," Cassidy put the little soldiers to one side and carried on rummaging. "The elf, the elf" laughed Maddy clapping her hands in delight at the little rag doll elf who always sat on the mantelpiece over the Christmas season, watching the children carefully, so it could report back to Santa whether they should be put on the naughty or nice list. Once the elf was reverently seated in the living room, I knew that the kids would behave as well as possible for the next few weeks of the year at least, even Toby still totally believed in it. Every year since we'd got together, Michael had bought me a small snow globe and they now adorned the top of the mantelpiece, next to Santa's spy. The tree was festooned with golden and red tinsel that shone in the glow of the twinkling multicoloured fairy

lights. Years of family memories hung from the branches in the shape of baubles, gingerbread men and reindeers and I couldn't decide whether I should have thrown everything out and started afresh, but it would have been like throwing out my children's childhood. Toby and Cassidy hung the candy canes and I was in no doubt that they wouldn't still all be there on the morning of the twenty fifth. A Christmas movie came on the telly and while we watched it, we made paper chain decorations to hang from the ceiling. The kids got a bit bored after a while and left me to it, whilst they played with the new 3D glasses they'd bought at Busy Bees. If you looked at any light source with them, you could see Santas in one set and gingerbread men in the other, it really was clever and kept them entertained for ages. Two bright red poinsettias were placed carefully at the bottom of the stairs, along with a dancing penguin and snowman. By the time I'd hung the paper chains and stowed the stepladders safely back in the cupboard under the stairs, the house was looking very festive. With the sun setting ever earlier, we kept the fairy lights on and by half past four in the evening, the only illumination inside the cottage, came from the fire and the lights on the tree, making our little home look like it was on the front of a Christmas Card. The kids were in Toby's room writing their letters to Santa, while I studded oranges with aromatic cloves and wrapped them with crimson ribbon, pondering over whether it was too early to crack open one of the big tins of chocolates I was saving for Christmas.

It wasn't just in the shops and our home that Christmas was making itself known, it was a busy time for us in school too. Having never worked in a school before I had no idea what a minefield casting for the school nativity could be. Although we'd spent five days of careful consideration before we'd decided on our Mary and Joseph, we'd still received six complaints from parents who thought their own child would be better suited to the roles. The saddest thing was the fact that at least two of those children whose parents had disagreed with our decision, wouldn't want the part anyway, they were far too shy to carry the lead role. Rehearsals were well underway and because it was a year group nativity, rather than a class one, we had to find parts for sixty children, so there were rather a lot of stable animals, quite a few angels and for the kids who couldn't be trusted with a part, they were in the choir. Whole lessons were abandoned in order to get the show into the unorganised debacle the parents would see and the PTA were in a state of near permanent anxiety, organising the annual Christmas Fair which was the biggest money spinner of the year, as I was reliably informed. I helped the children to paint the hats that they would proudly wear when eating their school Christmas dinners, which had proved to be an enjoyable task and even though we used water based paints, I still had to take three layers of skin off, before I could get rid of the red dye on my hands. We put the lights on ever earlier to combat the encroaching darkness of the wintry weather outside and every day you could see the kids becoming more excited, yet more exhausted as the term wore on, we were all sorely in need of a break. My days were so exclusively spent in preparation for Christmas, that I actually woke myself up in the night singing Christmas carols, it was easier to feel the magic of the season when you spent all your time in the company of very young children who whole heartedly believed in Santa, his elves and the naughty and nice list.

"I'm so sorry I can't come in today, I've been feeling nauseous all night, I feel terrible," I really hated lying, unless it was to my children to avert a crisis.

"No problem, hope you get better soon" answered my wonderful boss, without even a hint of suspicion in his voice. I'd had to wait until I'd taken the kids in to school, before I'd told Mr Matthews that I needed some time off sick, I couldn't risk one of the kids saying "no you haven't Mummy, you're fine." The truth was I needed a day off to go and buy all the Christmas presents for three children in one go because unfortunately, despite what they believed, I couldn't rely on Santa to deliver them the night before Christmas and I couldn't rely on Amazon to deliver them in time either. Another problem was that I didn't know the neighbours well enough yet to ask them to take in parcels for me whilst I was at school and even if they had, they would no doubt have come and knocked as soon as they saw the car there and then the kids would know something was up. So after considering all my options, I realised that lying was the only way I could ensure the magic on Christmas morning. I managed to get the last parking space in the whole of Newport and armed with the kid's Christmas lists that they'd helpfully written out for me, (and by me I meant Santa obviously) I set off to do battle. By half past one, I was seated in a cramped

Starbucks, relaxing with the largest Gingerbread Latte they offered, swamped by carrier bags and breathing a huge sigh of relief, that my work was done. The problem with shopping in the winter, was that the shops liked to keep their staff warm, but the poor shoppers had to wrap up in their jumpers and coats, so by the time you'd been in a queue for ten minutes, you were just about ready to faint. I may have gone a little overboard with the presents this year, but after the annus horribilis we'd just survived, I felt that they deserved it more than ever and a house on the island had cost considerably less than my share of the house in Bath. Supping my favourite Christmas tipple, I rejoiced in the freedom to buy the kids whatever I wanted to get them, without it descending into an argument, as it had every year. The problem was that I thought anything under fifteen presents each was depriving them and Michael thought that anything over one present each was spoiling them. Every year he'd set me a limit of one hundred pounds each and every year I'd gone way over it. I'd hide the presents so he didn't know what I'd done and every Christmas morning, the kids' faces would be a picture of happiness and excitement and his would be a mask of anger and bitterness. Every Christmas night, when the kids had fallen into an exhausted but happy sleep, instead of indulging in chocolate, a glass of Baileys and a Christmas special on TV like other couples, we'd end up having the mother of all arguments. The more I remembered from the past, the less I wanted to see him, but like it or not he was coming and I had to put the children's needs before my own, it really sucked to be a grown up sometimes.

I just had time to hide the presents in the loft, before it was time to go and collect the kids from school. To make myself look poorly I removed all of my make up in case anyone queried whether I was genuinely unwell and waited in the playground for my children to burst out of school at the end of the school day. Looking as pathetic as I possibly could, I deftly managed to avoid my boss and ushered the kids into the Audi as quickly as possible, it had been a necessity but I hadn't liked playing truant, I wasn't cut out for lying. "Can we go to McDonalds please Mummy?" Maddy asked, the traffic was unusually busy and after a hard days shopping, I had no desire to stand in the kitchen making food that three children didn't want to eat, so on seeing the smiles and the pleading looks aimed at me from the back seat, I willingly gave in.

As a general rule, the kids like to stay in the car and go through the drive-thru rather than having to eat a meal and deal with the general public at the same time. Five minutes later, Maddy was tucking into her fish finger meal. Cassidy had opted for chicken nuggets, Toby was enjoying his burger, which he always requested without any sauce, onions or pickle and I treated myself to a chicken sandwich. "Can I have some barbecue sauce for my chips please?" Maddy asked. Opening the little packet of sauce, I managed to splash some onto my pale blue jeans. "Damn it" I muttered, passing the sauce over to Maddy, "damn it, damn it" she repeated, like an ecstatic parrot. She always did have a gift for repeating the words you wouldn't want her to. I was just enjoying my chocolate milkshake, when Toby said "need the toilet" in a complete panic, trying to wrench open the car door. "Right everyone out, Toby needs to go." Any other child, you'd be able to say "go on and run on in" but Toby was going nowhere without me, no matter how desperate he was. We were just at the door when I heard a familiar voice shout out, "hello Natasha, feeling better ?" Turning in shock, I saw Dave Matthews standing behind me, with an equally beautiful man next to him, who I assumed was Tristan. I could feel myself turning beetroot red and I stood there gaping like a fish. "Yes a bit better thanks, I'll be back in tomorrow." Three suspicious eyes turned to stare at me, "are you ill Mummy ?" Maddy asked and I saw Dave's mouth twitching in amusement, but his eyes travelled downwards and he stopped smiling. Following his line of sight, I saw the brown smudge of barbecue sauce, standing out clearly on the pale blue of my jeans. "Oh it's just barbecue sauce" I laughed weekly, hoping the ground was going to open up and swallow me. "Mummy I've wet myself." We all turned to clearly see that Toby's school trousers were now very much darker at the top and streaks were making their way slowly down his legs. Brilliant, now Dave and his partner were under the impression that we were a family who suffered from raging incontinence. "Sorry, we've got to go, I'll see you tomorrow" without giving him a chance to reply, I yanked the door open and ushered the kids inside as swiftly as possible. It was without doubt, the most excruciatingly embarrassing moment of my life and if it wasn't for the kids I don't think I'd have left the McDonalds toilet cubicle. In bed that night, I tried to work out what had hurt the most, Dave seeing through my lie about being ill, having Dave think that I had possible faeces smeared across my jeans, Toby wetting himself in public, or the fact that I'd seen Dave and Tristan together, making his spectre of a boyfriend, suddenly all too real.

That night I dreamt that Tristan turned up on my doorstep crying, I'd invited him in and he'd sat on my sofa weeping that it was all over between himself and Dave, because after seeing us at McDonalds, Dave had confessed his true feelings for me and Tristan thought I should know, then he left the house and rode off on a tame lion he'd tethered to the gate outside the house. I was really going to have to stop having cheese on crackers before bed.

Chapter Ten

The longed for day had finally come. School was closed for the Christmas holidays and we were free for two whole weeks, unfortunately it also meant that Michael was due to arrive from Bath at any time. The school nativity had gone really well, even I'd been moved to tears at the sight of all the children in their little costumes and their proud parents taking photos, to be looked back on for years to come. Not wanting to remind Dave of our disastrous meeting, I'd described the young man I'd seen stood next to him in the McDonalds and Carole confirmed that it was indeed his boyfriend Tristan that had witnessed my humiliation. One lunchtime, he'd caught me feeling sorry for myself and I'd confided in him that I was dreading Michael coming over and how I'd only agreed to the visit for the kids' sake. He'd been a great listener and really sympathetic, leaving me feeling much better and I realised that having him as a friend might not be as good as having him for a boyfriend, but it came a pretty close second and over the last few days of term, I'd confided in him all the more.

Now that the day of Michael's visit was finally upon us, I found I was still dreading his imminent arrival, despite outward appearances. The kids had been unusually quiet and were secreted in their bedrooms where they'd been all morning. Every now and again I'd get calls for room service and found myself running up and down the stairs providing snacks and refreshments to three children who couldn't even look up from their tablets, when I brought them what they'd asked for.

My little living room had never looked so beautiful. The fire was roaring in the cast iron grate and the fairy lights twinkled brightly on the tree. I'd tried to distract myself by watching Home Alone on TV, but I kept pacing up and down every ten minutes or so, wondering when he was going to call, to say he'd arrived. It was bed time before I finally got a text saying, 'I've just checked in. Will see you tomorrow.'

"Damn him" I threw the phone onto the floor in disgust. I'd just spent the whole day waiting for him to arrive and he hadn't even had the common decency to let me and the kids know that he wasn't going to be seeing us straight away. If he was here on the island, why was he making us wait ? If he was trying to impress me, then these mind games weren't helping his cause. I went to tell the kids that they weren't going to be seeing their Dad until at least the morning, but they just nodded and carried on playing their game, linked together on their tablets. I truly didn't know what I would do, if we lost a tablet, Toby's was like his conjoined twin.

The temperature had fallen overnight and the radiators were on full blast, as well as the fire and inside, the house was warm and toasty, one of the benefits of living in a terraced home. I'd been up since six o'clock in the morning and as a result, every surface had been cleaned and polished until they shone. By the time the kids came downstairs, the fairy lights were twinkling once more and I had homemade doughnut batter ready to go and hot chocolates for everyone. "Are there anymore doughnuts ?" Maddy asked, licking the sugar off of her lips before drinking the remains of the chocolate. "Sorry hon, you've eaten six, I think that's enough don't you ?"

"No!" I didn't know where she puts it all, she could eat far more than me, when she put her mind to it. "Well that's all you're getting. It's time to go and get dressed."

"Whaaatttttt ?" Honestly, you'd think I'd just asked them to shoot a puppy in the face or something equally horrific. "Why ?" Toby's sugar high had obviously left him and he was back on the defensive. "I need you to get ready for when your Dad comes round." Well that was like a red rag to a bull and out of all of the kids, it was Maddy who I thought would want to see Michael the most, but it seemed I was wrong. Seconds later, she giggled and ran out of the living room and straight up the stairs. "Maddy" no answer, "Maddy come down here now." Still nothing. I climbed the stairs two at a time, with Toby and Cassidy following closely behind. Luckily, Maddy wasn't great at hiding, she worked on the theory that if she couldn't see you, then you couldn't possibly see her. So I found her sat on her bed, with a cardboard box on her head, thinking that she was the master of camouflage. "Maddy" I took the box gently off her head, "I told you I need you to get dressed."

"I'd love to, but I'm really very busy, I'll be happy to do it later though." I took a deep breath before I answered, I could hear my other two giggling behind the door. "I need you to do it now, I don't know what time he'll get here."

"I can't, I'm not well. I might be sick in a minute." Before I could insist, she burst into tears. The flood quickly abated, only to be replaced by anger and she started throwing her toys and screaming at me that she wasn't going to get dressed, before her grand finale where she threw herself on the floor waving her arms and legs around. "Okay Maddy, you win. If you don't want to get dressed you don't have to." The wailing subsided and I knew I at least had her interest. "I doubt if we could have got you ready before Cassidy gets dressed anyway, I just thought you would have liked to beat your sister at a competition that's all." Propelling herself off of the floor, Maddy raced to her wardrobe and started pulling out clothes. "Cassidy see if you can get dressed before Maddy. Go." I yelled, fortunately Cass was used to manipulating her sister and she yelled back "You'll never beat me." With a little bit of help, twenty minutes later, Cassidy was wearing jeggings and a pink fluffy jumper, Toby had on a Minecraft hoodie and a pair of jeans and Maddy was in jeggings, Peppa sweatshirt and an Iron Man mask.

My kids don't like waiting for anything and I wasn't about to send Michael a text, I wouldn't give him the satisfaction, so when the clock on the mantelpiece showed that it was ten o'clock in the morning, I nearly exploded with anger. "Right" I burst out, jumping off of the sofa, "let's go out."

"Are we going to see Daddy now ?" Iron Man asked expectantly, making me want to weep as I grabbed the coats, I really hated him for doing this. I should have told him he couldn't visit. We'd split our money evenly and he hadn't even mentioned any formal custody agreement, he'd been only too happy to skip off in the sunset with Janey to worry about visiting the kids, he'd thankfully been more interested in revelling in his new single status. The quickie divorce was going through uncontested, I supposed I should be thankful that this was the first time that he'd stopped playing ball, but it still rankled. "No darling, we're going to go to the pier in Sandown." All thoughts of their errant father were banished from their minds as they ran to the car, whooping and cheering in delight. I was just about to lock the front door, when I turned around feeling that something was wrong. "Where's Toby ?" The girls stood by the car looking innocent, well as innocent as Iron Man can look in his mask, at any rate. "Toby are you in there ?"

"Just coming" he was red in the face as he came running down the stairs. "What were you up to ?" Being a mum of children with very set routines and patterns I was instantly suspicion at any deviation in their habits. Toby didn't normally like being upstairs by himself and it was odd that he was suddenly sneaking up there alone. "Nothing, just grabbing my iPad." I was sure that he'd had his iPad on him all the time, but I wasn't definite enough to tackle him on it, so I let it go, but made a mental note to keep an eye on him all the same.

It was almost eleven o'clock and the children had spent seven pounds in two pence pieces trying

to win a key ring that would probably have cost fifty pence somewhere on the High Street, but Toby assured me it was the thrill of winning that made it worth me paying way over the odds for the piece of tat that would be forgotten come the morning. I'd been obsessively checking my phone signal all morning and as I fished it out of my bag once again, it started to ring in my hand. Not wishing to look too eager, I held it for a couple of seconds before answering, while three expectant children looked at me, trying to work out what I was doing. "Hello," I barked into the phone. I honestly didn't know how I'd managed to live in the same house with that man for so long, when I couldn't even answer the phone to him without feeling the need to have a shower. "Where are you ?" Not 'hi,' 'how're the kids ?' nothing, just straight in with an attack as though I should be sat around waiting for his call. "We're at Sandown Pier" I couldn't argue in public, with the children watching my every move.
"I'll be there in twenty minutes."
"Fine," I said shortly, relieved that he didn't want to meet at the house. The thought of him in my little safe space was too much to think about. It was cold and grey outside, so I didn't mind staying put for a while and the kids were having a good time, trying to win their key ring. My patience, much like the money in my purse was wearing thin, when I heard Cassidy murmur "there's Dad." Maddy, still in her superhero mask, shrieked "Daddy" and rushed off at a hundred miles an hour towards Michael, dangerously close to taking his legs out from under him. Any other dad, who hadn't seen his children for weeks, would have

scooped his daughter up, given her a hug and told her how much he'd missed her. Michael however, just stood there looking at her and said "Maddy, why are you wearing that mask ?" It had taken all of three seconds for him to ruin the atmosphere, it really was a gift. I noticed that Toby and Cassidy hadn't moved a muscle and were stood stiffly next to me, as Michael strode towards us with a devastated Maddy, holding her Iron Man mask listlessly in her hand. "Alright ?" He asked, as though he hadn't just hurt Maddy's feelings and was totally ignoring Toby and Cassidy. "I really need a coffee. Shall we go to the café at the back ?" Just as I had all through our marriage, I agreed to his decision, just trying to keep the peace, whilst simultaneously feeling defensive of my children and wanting to run away from him all over again. I refused to have anything to drink, so Michael stood in the queue to get a drink for him and the kids, whilst Maddy and I took one of the red and white painted seats and waited. Toby was staring out at the waves as they rushed to the shore and Cassidy had jammed her iPod into her ears, blotting out the awkwardness with pop music, as she often did. Out of the corner of my eye, I watched my ex-husband waiting impatiently for the drinks. His dark shoulder length hair was held firmly in place by whatever wax or mousse hair product he'd started using since I'd left him and he wore tight jeans that he wouldn't have ever worn before and a thick black woollen jumper. Janey had obviously been busy making her mark on him and I couldn't say that it was for the better. I'd never known the saying 'mutton dressed as lamb' to be applied to a man before, but that was definitely what Michael looked like now. I might even have felt sorry for him if he wasn't so bloody arrogant. "So how are you all ?" He was trying to make small talk but it felt like an interrogation. "We've got a new school Daddy" Maddy beamed, her mask abandoned on the bench beside her. "Do you like it ?" He asked, sipping his coffee. "Yes, Mummy works at Toby and Cassidy's school and I go to pre-school by myself because I'm a big girl, but when I'm an even bigger girl, I'm going to go to the same school too." Michael smiled, but I could tell he was annoyed that I hadn't told him I'd found myself a job, not that it had anything to do with him anymore, as Cassy would say 'obvs.' Toby had drank his lemonade down in one go and was starting to get restless with all the boring talk and having to sit still for more than three minutes, added to that, were his stress levels at seeing his dad again, so he started to flap his arms and bounce around, waiting for us to finish our drinks. I was used to Toby's little signals that he was heading for a breakdown, but Michael who never had any patience on these things, was instantly annoyed. He'd been experiencing an Autism free life for several weeks and his irritation was quick to surface. "Toby" he snapped, "stop it, everyone's looking at you." I actually felt my blood boil, as I watched Toby's mortified expression. "It's okay Tobes" I said soothingly, shooting Michael a withering glance, "it's only us up here anyway."

"I think that's hardly the point..." Michael began pompously, but he stopped when I leapt to my feet, grabbing the kids. "I think it's time we went, goodbye Michael." I thought I'd got away with it, thought we were free of him and in fact we were almost out of hearing range, when I heard him shout. "I'll see you later."

I don't know how I drove home, my hands were shaking so much in temper. How dare he belittle the kids, they had the whole world waiting to do that to them, we were their parents, we were the ones who should be protecting them and poor Cassidy, he hadn't even spoken to her at all. We spent the rest of the day watching Christmas movies on the sofa, with a thick blanket over our legs and I had a glass or three of mulled wine to calm my outraged nerves. I normally didn't drink the stuff, but it had been a present from a parent to thank me for my hard work in class. It tasted bitter but the scent was pure Christmas and it had alcohol in it, so it would do. The kids hadn't mentioned the meeting with their father and I didn't want to raise the subject, when they were all calm, but his last words kept rolling around in my mind, they'd definitely been meant as a threat. I just hoped he would think better of it, get back on the ferry and disappear back to Bath, out of our lives forever.

Every now and again Toby would run upstairs and come down again a few seconds later, when I tackled him about it, he said he had the feeling he needed to go to the toilet, but every time he got there, he realised he didn't. Toby's body didn't tell him when he needed to use the toilet very well and it's quite a humiliating thing for him to talk about, so I didn't press it, but I couldn't help but feel that he wasn't telling me the truth.

Later, when the kids were fast asleep, I went downstairs to steal some of their chocolate out of the fridge, justifying my actions that I was saving them from tooth decay and child obesity, when I heard a really loud banging that made me jump in terror. I ran to the front door and putting the security chain on first, I slowly opened the door. "Let me in" it was Michael and he was extremely drunk.

"Sssh" I admonished, "the kids are asleep and you know they don't stay that way for long. Go and sleep this off. Michael, we'll talk tomorrow." I tried to close the door, but he kept his foot in the way, so I couldn't shut him out. "You're my wife and you're keeping the chain on. Let me in." He was unsteady on his feet and the smell of alcohol poured off him in waves, making me curl my lip in disgust. "You'll frighten the kids."

"Typical you" he goaded "always worried about what the kids will think, always smothering them." "Keep your voice down." I tried desperately not to rise to the insults. "I'm not going to let you in, so go back and sober up." He began sobbing and it caught me completely off guard. "I just want you to come home. You've made your point now, but please come home. I've finished it with Janey." He'd never looked so unattractive as he stood swaying in the dark, illuminated by the light from my passageway, his eyes glassy and red, wiping his nose with the cuff of his coat. "Michael" I whispered, trying not to sound overly harsh, "I AM home, I'm not going anywhere. I'm happy here with the kids." He stumbled backwards, losing his footing and I just managed to slam the door on him before he had a chance to recover. I held my breath, waiting for him to start banging again, but thankfully he didn't, so after a few

minutes, I crept up to the safety of my bed. I lay down on the freezing cold sheets alone for all of ten seconds, when Cassidy appeared in the doorway. "Mum, was that Dad ?" She asked, crossing over to come and get in bed beside me. "Yes, he's gone back to his hotel now though, he was just here to say goodnight. Anyway, you should be asleep poppet"
"I'd sleep a lot easier if my drunken father wasn't trying to bang the door down." She raised an eyebrow at me that said, 'don't try and lie to me, I know everything' and cuddled down next to me in bed. She fell asleep a lot quicker than I did.

Chapter Eleven

"Mum... phone." My kids liked to tell me when the phone was ringing, just in case the loud ringing sound emitting from the telephone in short pulses wasn't enough to alert my attention. Not that any of them would ever dare to answer it for me, after all they might have to speak to a real person and none of them were willing to take that risk, Toby had once explained to me that saying 'Hello' to someone was the start of an unknown conversation where he didn't know what to say after, almost the same as if you were in France and all you knew was the word 'bonjour' and once you said it to someone they would assume you could speak French and then would start jabbering away at you in a language you didn't understand. The cause of all the excitement was the fact that it was the house phone ringing and not the mobile. No one ever rang the house phone except for salesmen and on the very odd occasion my mother and quite frankly I was rather hoping it was the former rather than the latter, on the other end. I only had the thing in case the kids were ill during the night and I couldn't get a signal. "Hello." I'd only just succeeded in grabbing the receiver before it went into answer phone. "Hello Natasha, it's Beryl." Well, that was a conversation killer if ever I'd heard one. I put my fingers to my lips, warning the

kids to keep quiet and closed my eyes. If there was one person I hadn't expected to hear from, it was my mother in law Beryl. "To what do I owe this honour ?" In all the years of our marriage Beryl had never called to speak to me or the children, but always to speak to her special little prince, so I had no qualms over my sarcastic greeting, luckily she had the skin of a rhinoceros and didn't even seem to notice my tone. "I'm ringing about Michael." I started to panic, what if something had happened to him after I'd slammed the door on him and refused to move back to Bath ? What if he'd had an accident... or worse ? What would I tell the kids. "What's wrong ?" I tried to keep the trembling out of my voice as I looked across at the three kids who were obliviously watching one of their favourite cartoon programmes, not even remotely interested in who I might be speaking to. "You need to give him a chance. You need to stop this foolishness and come back to Bath and be a wife again." I was stunned and not altogether sure whether this was an order or request. "I'm sorry ?" A small kernel of outrage was growing in the pit of my stomach. "Those children need their father and you're keeping them away from him."
"I'm sorry Beryl, but this has nothing to do with you." I was ready to slam the phone down on her, but my mother in law wasn't finished with me just yet. "It has everything to do with me," she retorted, raising her voice, she wasn't used to being ignored. "I'm the one that has to hear him crying on the phone to me every night. He misses you."

"Well I'm very sorry about that, but it's not so simple, one day I hope you'll understand, but I can't talk about it at the moment. Bye Beryl."

The tinsel sparkled soothingly and the little living room was so snug, this was our home now and there was no way I would trade this in to go back to Bath, back to Michael. The kids were beginning to settle into their new life and we were happier as a result, but something in Beryl's words had rattled me. What if it wasn't in the kids' best interests to be here ? What if I had been too hard on Michael ? What if I was being too over protective and had pushed my husband away in the process ? What if all dads found it hard to understand Asperger's and PDA ? Had I uprooted the family and left my husband on a whim ? Was it the fact that I wasn't often in the mood to make love, my fault ? Had he been right, was there something wrong with me ? Should I have gone to see the doctor like Michael suggested at the time ? Was I the cause of his anger and animosity to the children ? All these thoughts ran depressingly through my mind, but it was Christmas Eve and I had no intention of letting anyone ruin our first Christmas, Michael should be halfway back to Bath by now anyway and it would thankfully just be us until my mum and John arrived.

"Mum it's snowing…. It's snowing," Cassidy was beside herself with excitement. Within minutes, the kids were all assembled with their coats and hats on ready to go and play in the snow, especially Maddy who was dressed like Captain America on an Antarctic expedition, they'd never put their coats on so quickly by themselves before. The small flakes had turned into large white fluffy flakes of snow obscuring the ground, making our garden look even more like a Christmas card. "Don't get too cold" I shouted, as Captain America disappeared through the back door behind her brother and sister, leaving a cold gust of wind in her wake. I made myself a coffee and kept an eye on them, whilst frequently nipping back into the living room to pinch one of the little chocolates from the Santa shaped bowl next to the TV. As I watched them playing, through the window, I questioned my judgment once again. The weight of being a parent was enormous sometimes and you never quite knew for sure whether you'd really made the right decision and to second guess yourself was wearing, but when you had your mother in law calling you and questioning the choices you'd made, it was difficult to see the bigger picture. Yet nothing in Michael's visit had made me think I could go back to him. In fact until Beryl's telephone call, he'd only reinforced my belief that I'd been in the right to move as far away from him as possible, but was his attitude just bravado ? Was he really crying to his mother every night ?

  The door burst open, letting in an icy blast and three children flew back in, their cheeks and noses glowing red and their hands and feet were blue and frozen. "Come on, in front of the fire, let's get you out of those clothes." As they started to thaw, I got them into warm dry clothes and they sat happily in front of the blazing fire. "Who wants hot chocolate ?" I didn't get very far, before Maddy grabbed me firmly around the legs, holding me in place, "I love it here Mummy, it's snowing on Christmas Eve. It never snowed in Bath on Christmas did it ?"

"No honey" I laughed, "it didn't." I'd just been worrying myself about whether the kids were upset at being uprooted, but apparently they didn't need their father or their old friends to make them feel happy, they just needed some snow and the large rather scary looking snowman in the garden was proof of that. It was nice to see that they'd done something together in the real world, normally they only cooperated when they were linked via their tablets.

The hot chocolates were passed around and they were quite happy eating their way through a large tin of chocolates and watching the various Christmas specials on TV, it really was blissful. As I looked up my gaze was caught by the strings of Christmas cards they had received from their new friends at school and the two I had received, one from the gossipy Carole and the other from Dave, it was a start and I was hopeful for the New Year to come.

We were just watching a TV pantomime starring several washed up celebrities and a sprinkling of nauseatingly nice kid's TV presenters, when there was a thunderous pounding on the door. The snow hadn't let up all day and only a fool would be out and about in this weather on Christmas Eve, I knew it wasn't the postman because he'd already delivered some bills earlier in the day, which still remained on the side unopened. The kids jumped in fright at the noise, "it's okay, I'll go and see who it is." I opened the door, thinking it would be one of the neighbours who'd locked themselves out or had lost their dog or something, but I realised too late that it was Michael. He was in the hallway, before I could stop him and I cursed myself for not securing the chain first, I would have done if I hadn't honestly believed that he'd be back in Bath by now. "Tash, I need to see the kids before I go." Snow covered his immaculate hair and the shoulders of his thick navy pea coat. He was unshaven and looked so tired that despite my inner alarm sounding, I couldn't ignore his imploring look and relented, at least once he'd said goodbye, he would be gone and we could carry on with our perfect little Christmas. "How would you like to come home to Bath and spend Christmas Day with Daddy and your Gran ? We could see some of your old friends too. I think Santa might be a bit confused, he might deliver your presents to our old house, he might think this is just your holiday home and besides I'd be lonely without you on Christmas Day." I was gob smacked, how could he ? He'd managed to undermine our new home and our Christmas plans in one go, he hadn't even had the decency to talk it over with me first, I hated him in that moment, but I stood frozen, waiting for the kids' response. I didn't want to emotionally manipulate them, there'd been enough of that from their father. "We can spend Christmas with you Daddy" Maddy said looking around uncertainly, the other two nodded in mute agreement. "But what about the weather ? It's snowing outside, I don't think you should go," I blurted out, unable to keep silent any longer. "Stop fussing, they'll be fine."

Five minutes later, the kids were waiting in the hallway, with their bags packed, "oh I nearly forgot," Maddy disappeared into the living room, coming back out a couple of minutes later with Michael's Christmas stocking in her hand. "We have to take this back to Bath Daddy" she said solemnly, handing him the years old red velvet stocking. I was still stunned, unable to believe it was really happening and powerless to stop it. My face was a rigid mask, as I desperately tried not to let the tears fall. "When will you bring them back ?" I asked through gritted teeth, mortified at the weakness in my voice, but I still had enough pride left not to beg. "I'll drop them off on Boxing Day. Say goodbye to your Mother kids." I dropped to my knees as they each gave me a kiss and silently followed him out to the car. I waited until I heard his car pull away, before I allowed the tears to fall and lay on the hallway floor wailing, sobbing my heart out for my three beautiful children.

Eventually, I made my way to the sofa and pulling the blanket over me, I lay in the dark, staring blankly at the fairy lights, unsure what to do, now that Christmas had been ruined. I knew that when they came back on Boxing Day, I couldn't make them feel guilty for choosing to go with their Dad and we'd have our Christmas celebrations then, but in the meantime I was happy to stay on the sofa feeling sorry for myself, licking my wounds. Everything in me had wanted to stop them from leaving, but I wasn't going to stoop to his level, it had to be their decision. Using Santa and loneliness had been a low move.

I'd just started to doze off when I my mobile burst into life, grabbing it in confusion, I didn't even look to see who was calling, I pushed it against my ear. "Hello ?" I didn't even know what the time was, but through the open curtains, I could see that it was pitch black outside the windows. "I've lost the kids." Four words, that was all it needed to make my heart stop beating. "What do you mean you've lost the kids ?" I shrieked, leaping up to put my shoes on. "I'll explain when you get here." He was acting like this was all my fault. "Where are you ?" I already had the keys in my hand, heading out of the door. "I'm in Yarmouth."

"Yarmouth ? That's the other side of the bloody island." This was getting worse by the minute, everything outside the house seemed muted by the thick blanket of snow, glowing a strange orange in the haze of the street lights, making my voice carry farther than usual. "Yes Yarmouth, it's the quickest crossing back to home."

"Right. Where did you lose them ?"

"I told you. I'll explain when you get here. The people at the port have contacted the police."

"Keep me informed if anything changes." Luckily, as it was Christmas Eve and the snow was still falling, the roads were unnaturally quiet. I drove as fast as I dared to go, I didn't want to end up in a ditch while my kids were out there somewhere in the cold dark night. I actually wondered whether I was dreaming and this was all some sort of horrendous nightmare, or a tasteless practical joke and I'd get to the port and Michael would be there with the kids, laughing at the prank they'd pulled on me. All my suspicions were swept away and I knew it was really happening, when I got to Yarmouth and saw the blue flashing lights illuminating the ferry port.

"What happened ?" I asked my gormless ex as he stood talking to a policeman by the side of the

jetty. The police car lights flashing on the walls of Yarmouth Castle made a few revellers from the George Hotel next door, venture outside to find out what was going on. "I pulled up here to wait for the ferry and Maddy said she needed the toilet. Toby and Cassidy said they'd go with her."
"Wait a minute, you let them go off by themselves ? Where were you ?"
"I stayed in the car, I had a phone call. For Christ's sake Tash. Toby's ten now."
"He's NINE actually" I spat back in disgust, making the policeman look uncomfortable, while Michael glared at me with a 'whatever' look on his face. "Then what happened ?"
"Well they'd been gone for ages and when I went to look for them they were gone."
"Oh my God, my babies have been kidnapped." My head spun as I gasped for air. "Not necessarily" the thin nervous looking policeman with a thick moustache interjected. "What do you mean ?" There was obviously more going on than anyone had told me. "The children were seen walking out of the building of their own accord, by a member of staff."
"So how did you not see them ? The car is facing the exit door."
"I told you I was.. Er… taking a call." Every question seemed to annoy him, in fact he didn't appear to be worried about the kids at all, just annoyed that his ferry had left and he was being inconvenienced by recent events. "Who were you talking to ?" I noticed he wouldn't look at me and thrust his hands deep into his pockets as he answered. "I was talking to Janey if you must know. We've decided to make a go of things,

she's waiting at home for me." I rubbed my hands against my eyes, trying to blot out the anger that was threatening to transform into a migraine and I tried to weigh up whether I could claim provocation if I attacked him, but that wasn't going to help me find my children. "Why would they have run off ? What did you do ?"

"Nothing." I'd known him for too long not to know when he was keeping something from me. "Michael, our kids are out there somewhere in this snow. If you know something then you have to tell me."

"Okay, I shouted at them alright. Happy now?"

"The kids are missing, Michael so no, I'm far from happy. What did you shout at them for ?"

"Maddy got upset and wanted to go back for a stupid costume. I told her we had to get the ferry and there wasn't time, she kicked off and I shouted at her to be quiet. You've really let them get away with murder, since you brought them here, they're completely out of control." I ground my teeth, ignoring the jibe.

"Then what happened ?" I watched the ferry that my family should have been on, at the other side of The Solent just putting into Lymington, while its sister ship made its way steadily back across towards Yarmouth. "Toby started saying that I was always shouting and he didn't like the noise."

"What did you say ?" I could pretty much guess what his response was.

"I told him that I was the adult and I would speak to him or Maddy or Cassidy however I wanted and that he should shut up."

"Has he told you that two of the children have Asperger's Syndrome and one also has

Pathological Demand Avoidance ?" I asked the policeman, who was busily jotting down everything Michael had said. "No madam, he didn't," I glared at my ex in disgust. "They're very vulnerable and to be honest its no wonder that they ran away from him, I've only just done it myself and it was the best thing I've ever done."
"Do you know what Tash, I'm so fed up of this." The policeman and I stood quietly, wondering what on earth he was going to say next. "You keep excusing everything on their 'Autism.' I've had enough of them and you. I just wanted normal kids, but you've put this thing in their heads and I feel like I'm treading on bloody eggshells all the time. I can't deal with this. You've all got your wish, I'm going home, I'll leave you all alone, I'm going to make a go of it with Janey and have a quiet life, she doesn't want to deal with this baggage either." As angry as I was, especially when he'd mimed air quotes when he'd said the word Autism and called my kids baggage, I'd had enough too. "I think it's for the best. Just go." Sheepishly he got into the car, slamming the door behind him, waiting for his ferry. "Well that's just unbelievable" the policeman gave a low whistle of disbelief. "What happens now ?" I just wanted to concentrate on finding the kids, the snow was coming down pretty heavily now. "We've alerted police across the island and I've got colleagues making enquiries around Yarmouth. There aren't many people around, but in this weather, three children would be more noticeable, walking around on their own to anyone who saw them."
"What should I do ?"

"Is there anyone they would go to for help, or anywhere they might want to visit ?"

"No, we've only just moved here, there's nowhere that I can think of."

"Your husband gave us your number, the best thing you can do is to return home and wait to find out if they turn up there, most missing children will make their way home following an argument, once they think their parents have been suitably punished. We'll keep searching for them here." Numbly, I nodded at the policeman and accepting his assurances that they would call me as soon as they had any news, I took one last look at Michael's car, waiting in the queue for the ferry and sped off in the direction of home.

I'd only been home a matter of minutes, when the house phone rang, I grabbed at it, hoping against hope that it would be some good news. "Hi Natasha, it's Dave," said a cheery voice at the end of the line, my stomach rolled in disappointment. "Dave, I can't talk on the phone, I'm waiting for the police to call." I wanted to cry at the feelings of hope he'd inadvertently dashed. "What's wrong ?"

"The kids have gone missing."

"I'm coming round."

"No it's fine, you don't need…" He'd already put the phone down. Fifteen minutes later, I heard a loud knocking on the front door. I knew it wouldn't be the kids, making such a racket, but just to see a friendly face reduced me to a sobbing mess and I collapsed in his arms.

He made me a cup of strong coffee as I poured out the nights events, he didn't pass comment, he simply nodded, listening to everything, though his

mouth tightened almost imperceptibly when I got to the part where Michael had shouted at the kids. "Is there nowhere you can think of that they might go ?" I shook my head, wiping away the tears, placing the coffee on the table next to me. "No, none at all. They don't even know the island that well, they must be so scared. I could kill Michael for this."
"I can't believe he's just left, not knowing where his kids are."
"To be honest, nothing he does surprises me anymore. I'm just glad he's gone and he's going to leave us alone... Oh God where are my children ? I feel so helpless doing nothing." He put his arm around me as I sobbed and I realised how much I'd missed having someone to confide in, to hold me when I was at my lowest ebb. I sat staring into the fire, imagining all sorts of horrifying scenarios involving my children, when the mobile rang. It was a number I didn't recognise and the woman on the other end was whispering, making her difficult to hear. "Is this Toby's mum ?"
"Yes ?" I stared quizzically at Dave, who sat staring at me in return, with his fingers crossed, hoping for good news. "Hi, its Melody's mum." I was silent, the name meant nothing to me. "Your children are here, I thought at first Toby was just visiting, but I overheard him talking about running away and they seemed very cold when they got here. Toby doesn't know I've called you, I got your number from the mobile phone in his bag." I nearly dropped the phone in relief, I wanted to sob, but this wasn't the time. "Where are you ?"

    She gave me her address in Brading and promised to keep the kids with her until I got there. As I drove, Dave called the police and informed them that the children had been found and they promised to call at the house in an hour or so to ensure that the kids were safe and well. I didn't even bother to call Michael to let him know.

I knocked lightly on the door, of a little terraced cottage opposite The Bugle pub in Brading and was met by the friendly face of a middle aged blonde woman. Ever since we'd spoken, I had been flooded with relief but I was also confused about who Melody was and why my children had run to her house, instead of home to me. The lady ushered me into a tiny little living room, where my children were sat around a TV, with a young blonde haired girl with huge blue eyes, beneath thick black glasses who was the spitting image of her mother and I presumed that was Melody. My children looked shocked to see me, then really surprised to see Mr Matthews behind me and then accusingly at Melody's mother, who had obviously told on them. "It's okay" I assured them, edging my way onto the sofa. "I'm just glad you're okay, I've been really worried about you all."

"Daddy was horrible, I only wanted a super hero costume, so I could be a real super hero and look after him when he was sad, but he shouted at me." Maddy burst into tears and came to sit on my lap, putting her little arms around my neck and pressing herself into me. "I know sweetheart, I know. He's gone now and he's not coming back." It was a good job that he'd left the island, because if I ever saw him again, I couldn't be held responsible for my actions. "We only said we'd go

with him because he seemed so sad, but as soon as we left, he changed," put in Cassidy.
"I know, he told me all about it, I'm so sorry."
"Why's he here ?" Toby pointed to Dave, who so far hadn't said a word.
"I was worried about you mate" he said, "your Mum was really scared, so I've been looking after her."
"Mummy needs someone to look after her" announced Maddy, wiping her snotty nose in my neck and I held her close, determined never to let her go again. "Why did you come here ?" I didn't want to sound unappreciative, but I was really confused. "Melody's my girlfriend" Toby said all matter of fact. "We've been texting one another," so that explained his frequent disappearing acts upstairs, he'd been sending messages to his girlfriend and I realised she was the girl he'd been sat at lunch with on his first day at school. "We didn't want to come home in case Dad was there and we didn't know what to do."
"But how did you even get here, you were over in Yarmouth ?" Cassidy and Melody looked sheepishly at the floor, but Toby was uncharacteristically proud of himself. "When I was in my room, before we left, I took all my savings with me, just in case we needed it and while Daddy was busy on the phone we ran past the car and found a taxi."
"Well Tobes" I tried to smile at him. "I'm really glad you have a girlfriend and I'm really pleased that you've been well looked after, but it's Christmas Eve and I think it's time for us to go home and let Melody's family have their house back, don't you." I thanked Melody's mum and

promised to keep in touch before I drove the kids and Dave back home in the Audi.

The police came shortly after our arrival and after talking to the children, who were rather revelling in the drama, they left, happy that the children were no longer a flight risk and hadn't been too traumatised by the whole event. I left Dave in front of the fire, watching an old rerun of the Two Ronnies and took the children up to bed, after putting out a mince pie, a carrot and a glass of milk for Santa and the reindeer first of course. I got them to clean their teeth without fuss, they were being cooperative, because they didn't want to be on the naughty list and running away couldn't exactly guarantee them a place on the nice list, so they were doing everything in their power to make amends. After the shock of the evening, I allowed them to snuggle up in my bed together and kissed them all goodnight. "We don't have to see Daddy again do we ?" Maddy asked as I started to creep out the door. "No sweetheart you definitely don't," I assured her.

"Mummy, we like Mr Matthews."

"That's good honey, now get to sleep, otherwise Santa won't bring your presents will he ?" That was enough to get her to lie back down and I softly closed the door, thankful that they were all okay and Michael was out of our lives now for good.

Tiptoeing back down the stairs, I was filled with such thankfulness that I had a friend waiting on the sofa for me, after months of no adult company in the evening. He was more concerned about the children than their own father was, I was lucky to have a friend like him. He was even spending

Christmas Eve in my living room, instead of out partying with Tristan. At the thought of his partner I suddenly felt guilty that I was taking up all of his time, "shouldn't you be going ?" I didn't mean it to sound as harsh as it had come out, but I could tell by the way his cheeks reddened and he stuttered, that I'd made him feel uncomfortable and he awkwardly reached for his coat that was drying on the back of a chair. "Right yes, well, I'm just glad that you're all okay."
"Yeah, thanks for everything, I really don't know what I would have done without you." We stood in the doorway, the snow falling behind him and the streetlights illuminating him in a golden orange halo, he looked like he was about to say something, but seemed to think better of it and grabbed his keys out of his pocket, ready to leave. He was so perfect, it made me want to cry. "Merry Christmas Natasha" he whispered as he stepped out into the night. "Merry Christmas Dave." I had to let him know that I knew his secret, that it was okay to confide in me after all we'd been through, he'd just spent the worst night of my life with me, supporting me, when none of it had been his problem. "I hope Tristan's not too mad that you've been here all this time on Christmas Eve. Carole told me at work, please don't be cross, I won't say anything to anyone." He held my gaze with a loaded look for a few seconds, before turning and getting into his car that was mostly obscured by snow. I shut the door and went to bed, it had been a long day.

Chapter Twelve

Christmas Day was absolute bliss, I'd even go so far as to say that it was the best one I'd ever had, even better than the year I'd got my much loved Cabbage Patch Doll, that was now forgotten in a box, somewhere in the attic because I'm too old to play with 'Brittany Tammy,' but couldn't bear to part with her after all this time, especially after everything we'd gone through together when I was little and after I saw that really sad bit in Toy Story 2 when the doll gets left behind in a cardboard box when the girl grows up, I couldn't do that to my beloved 'adopted daughter doll.' After the unwrapping of presents, I cleared away the piles of discarded wrapping paper and tried to make a pathway through the living room, which was completely littered with toys and boxes.

While the kids happily played, I made them the usual breakfast of bacon and pancakes that we'd always started Christmas mornings with. Maple syrup was the only liquid that Toby would permit to touch his food and so they wolfed their breakfast down without the usual complaints, before hurrying back to play with their new toys. The fresh turkey from the butcher in Shanklin was cooking nicely in the oven, the vegetables were bubbling away, the kilted sausages, stuffing and roast potatoes were nearly done to perfection and

all I had left to do was to pop the Yorkshire puddings in. The little dining table in the corner of the living room looked resplendent with a Christmassy tablecloth, festive penguin shaped plates for the kids, Santa napkins and the obligatory Christmas crackers next to each set of cutlery. The kids were in a great mood and even ate most of their food without grumbling, although only Cassidy asked for gravy on hers and they all ignored the sprouts, which I couldn't really blame them for, I didn't have any either, but it's Christmas and you have to at least have them on the table at Christmas. We all sat with our party hats on, though there was a little bit of a squabble when Toby saw that Maddy had a red hat and red was his favourite colour, so after a bit of negotiation, everyone was happy and I was a pound down, due to bribery. The snow had stopped falling, but the snowman still stood proudly and slightly malevolently in the garden watching the house and every now and again I found myself staring out of the kitchen window, to see whether he'd moved any nearer towards the back door. "Mummy what did you want for Christmas ?" Maddy broke into my thoughts as I put the clean plates back in the cupboard.
"Nothing sweetheart, I've got everything I need right here, I have you, Tobes and Cass, what more could I want ?"
"What about a boyfriend ?"
"Don't be silly" said Toby, walking into the kitchen behind her, no doubt on the lookout for more turkey. "You have to wish for love on Valentine's Day, not at Christmas."

Maddy was incensed, "that's not true is it Mummy?"

"It doesn't matter sweetheart, I'm not looking for a boyfriend." I tried to usher them back into the living room where I could distract them with their presents. "What about Mr Matthews, I thought you liked him?" Now Cassidy was joining the 'get Mummy a boyfriend gang.' "I do like him, but he's a friend that's all. He's already got someone he's in love with anyway," that seemed to kill the conversation and they settled back down to playing their new computer games on their handheld consoles, leaving me to relax in front of the TV with a whole chocolate orange to myself, now I really did have everything I needed.

Boxing Day morning was very much the morning after the night before. My lovely little clean and tidy house looked like a bomb had hit it. Even though I'd followed the kids around, clearing up after them, it was still full of stray bits of wrapping paper, empty boxes and half eaten chocolate and sweets that had been tried and then discarded. Normally on Boxing Day I'd stay in my onesie, but I didn't have the luxury this time, my mother was about to arrive with her rich husband and as it was the first time they'd seen our new home, I was determined not to give her any reason to look down her nose at our little palace. I begged the kids to stay in their bedrooms whilst I tidied from top to bottom, we'd just got ourselves looking presentable when there was an impatient knocking on the front door.

Flying down over the stairs, the kids wrenched open the door before I could get to it and hugged my mother. "Hello, hello" she smiled, "let me get in, it's been a long journey." Once my mother had settled herself down on the sofa and had a cup of hot sweet tea in her hand, she allowed the children to show her what they'd been given for Christmas and then made John go to the car, bringing a large sack of presents back into the house with him. The sack full of presents they'd received on Christmas Day had not diminished their appetite for more presents in the least and within minutes my living room floor was once more hidden beneath a pile of torn wrapping paper. "Thank you mother," I smiled, handing her over a wrapped tin of shortbread biscuits I'd picked up in Marks' in Newport when I'd played truant from school. I always bought her the same thing, if I ever showed initiative and surprised her, whatever I'd bought would be promptly returned and she'd go and buy herself some shortbread with the money instead.

The day passed in a whirl of the kids proudly showing off their presents to my mother and John and them politely nodding in feigned interest, but as long as I kept refilling her glass with gin, my mother kept the smile on her face. Eventually the kids retreated to their rooms, leaving the grown-ups to the Christmas TV.

My mother always insisted on us having red salmon with salad for Boxing Day and so I ended up in the kitchen, preparing food whilst my mother and step father watched an old Indiana Jones film in the living room. As usual I had to make different meals to accommodate everyone and I knew my mother wouldn't approve of me being so flexible with the kids, but I didn't want to spend all of Boxing Day shut away, so I put pizzas in the oven for the kids and hoped that my mother would keep her opinions to herself.

Finally, when everything was ready, I laid out the spread on the small dining table and the kids were completely thrilled because with my mother and John visiting, there weren't enough seats, meaning that they could eat their food on the sofa for once, watching TV. "Well this looks nice I must say." My mother didn't hand out compliments very often, so it was a good start. We all seated ourselves down and I'd just raised the fork to my mouth, feeling relaxed for the first time in days, when my mother, putting her empty gin glass down, looked at me sternly across the table and said "Beryl called me." My fork clattered onto my plate, spilling salmon and beetroot juice all across my very best white tablecloth. "I don't think now's the time to talk about it, do you ?" I nodded towards the children, talking without moving my mouth like a prize winning ventriloquist. "Nonsense dear" undermining me as usual, I suddenly remembered why I'd been so glad to move away. "Beryl called and said that Michael was making a go of things with Janey and his visit here had been a complete disaster. He said you were completely unreasonable."
"Mother, I must insist." I was perilously close to banishing her from the house, the kids had been through enough already, they didn't need to hear my mother's biased opinion. "I don't know why you left him I really don't." Her ability to be so completely oblivious to everyone else's feelings completely astounded me, the paediatrician had told me that the children's Asperger's was probably genetic and looking at my mother, I was

certain that she was the immediate source. I couldn't tell her, when the kids were listening that Michael had never understood them, never believed their diagnoses and had been a terrible father and caused them to run away, even leaving the island without calling to check that they were safe and well. I couldn't let them think that any of this was their fault, so I was forced to bite my lip against the tsunami of criticism flowing my way instead. "I had my reasons and anyway it's all over now."

"Daddy was mean to us and we ran away," Maddy piped up, suddenly entering the conversation with her mouth full of her last bite of pizza. "Come on," Cassidy said gently, "let's go up and play Toby's new Sonic game." Sensing that something was wrong, Maddy followed her brother and sister without argument as I held my breath, trying not to explode with anger at my mother. Once I was sure the kids were safely out of earshot, I stood with my hands planted firmly on the table in front of me, facing my mother in a way I'd never dared to before. "I left for the sake of my children, because he couldn't accept them for who they were." She tutted and rolled her eyes at me in her immaculately painted face. Her light blonde perfectly straightened hair lay on her shoulders and her navy linen trousers and red striped Joules sweater made me feel as though I'd been dragged through a hedge backwards, even in an argument she was still cool and detached, completely unruffled. I knew my hair was standing on end and I was red in the face, but for once I didn't care. I'd spent my whole life being a good daughter, never talking back, never saying what I felt and all I'd got was stomach problems from all the bitterness I'd had to swallow and my mother didn't respect me any the more for it, I'd finally had enough. It was time to tell the old woman some home truths. "Despite what you might think, my children have been diagnosed by qualified professionals, they have their problems and they need the right environment to thrive in. Michael was bad for them and he proved that, when he shouted at them and they ran away. For God's sake he got on that ferry and went home before even finding out if they were okay and I will NEVER forgive him for that. He only told his mother that it was all my fault, because he's a coward who doesn't want to see the kids anymore and they don't want to see him and for that matter neither do I and if you can't understand that, then feel free to join him." The silence was deafening, I could hear the kids playing upstairs and breathed a sigh of relief that they hadn't been listening outside the door. Even this turn in events only silenced my mother for a couple of seconds and she opened her mouth to reply, but John cut in, preventing her from saying something she'd regret. "I think that Natasha has proved herself to be a fantastic mother and whatever she's decided will be what's best for her children. We should support her and toast her in her new life, with a gin, don't you ?" My mother's anger was instantly subdued and she nodded in mute agreement, John didn't get the chance to speak much, but when my mother let him, he was usually the voice of reason and I smiled my thanks at him, as he strode off into the kitchen to fix some more drinks.

The rest of the day passed in polite companionship, we even talked the kids into playing a few games of charades, before bed. I put them to bed in their own rooms, while I eased myself into a sleeping bag on the sofa with the TV on mute. I could hear my mother snoring in my bed above me and giggled at the thought of a confused Maddy bursting into the bedroom at two in the morning, when she woke up and forgot that we had guests. My mother also wouldn't be used to everyone being awake at six thirty in the morning either.

Chapter Thirteen

My mother and step father left for the ferry port at Fishbourne first thing on New Year's Eve. I waved them goodbye with a sense of relief, but a calmness too. John's intervention had clearly had a profound effect on my mother and she had been a different person for the remainder of her stay, not necessarily understanding, but definitely less critical and that was a blessing. We'd ventured out into the snow for a meal at the Vine Inn and my mother had even talked the kids into a drive into Ryde and they'd ran over the snow covered sand, chucking snowballs at one another, until Maddy caught one in the eye and started to cry. I know my mum and step father are family, but it felt too much like I was having to entertain them, as though I were running a bed and breakfast and I'd tried hard to maintain the fragile goodwill we were finally experiencing, so it felt like they'd been with us for weeks rather than a few days. I desperately hoped that my mother wouldn't feel the need to return to the island anytime soon, but I was pleased that we'd at least parted on good terms and we finally had our house back.

While Cassidy and Maddy made some charm bracelets and Toby played on his iPad, I changed the bedding on all the beds trying to make the house feel like ours again. The Christmas holidays would soon be at an end, school would reopen and we'd get back into our routine and our life would continue as normal, in our new home. At least Christmas had proved beyond a shadow of a doubt that I'd made the right decision to move here.

We'd just had lunch, when I heard the letterbox rattle, thinking it was probably just bills I ignored it, but Toby couldn't stand not investigating and ran off to find out what lay inside the envelopes on the welcome mat. "Here you are Mum" he shoved the post at me, watching intently as I quickly flicked through them, I'm not sure what he thinks will come in the post, an invite to Buckingham Palace or something ? Two were credit card bills from companies who actually had found a way to put a price on Christmas joy and the other was rather official looking. I ripped the last one open and pulling out the document inside, I produced my Decree Absolute. It was finished, my marriage was finally over. I could start the New Year completely free. I'd just filed my certificate of singledom into my metal file box where I kept things like birth certificates and all my important papers when I heard the letterbox go again. "Mummy... Mummy, come here quick." Sensing the urgency in Cassidy's voice I ran down the stairs two at a time, to find her holding two small books and a folded up piece of paper in her hands. One of the books a little blue leather bound one was a collection of poems by Keats and the other a red and gold one which looked expensive was by Alfred, Lord Tennyson. According to Toby's 'fun facts of the Isle of Wight lecture' both poets had once lived on the island and wrote romantic poetry. I read the word 'Natasha' in vaguely familiar handwriting and my stomach lurched in response, what if Michael hadn't got on the ferry after all ? "Let me see" I held out my hand, waiting and read the words written within. 'Turner once thought me worthy of painting and though I lie motionless, I am beautiful still.' "What does it say ?" asked Toby, as three children leaned over my arms desperate to read the cryptic note. "I can't read it" Maddy jumped up and down in frustration, dressed as she was in a Power Rangers outfit. "It's the Bembridge Windmill" declared Toby smugly.

"Are you sure ?" My son didn't appreciate being doubted, especially when he was almost always right. "Google it" he said with a withering glance and two minutes later, he was proved right, thanks to a brief online search. Toby of course knew all along and stood tapping his foot in disgust that we'd actually looked it up instead of trusting him, even though he was the absolute King of Mistrust. "Well done Tobes" I shook my head in amazement, "I don't know how you know all these amazing facts."

"Yeah Toby's clever, we know that" chipped in Cassidy. "What do we do now ?" My children had a way of cutting straight through to the truth, before I did. "I don't know."

"We go to the windmill of course." The red power ranger was already pulling on her wellie boots, closely followed by her brother and sister. "We don't know what's going on or who sent this, it could be anyone."

"Well let's go and find out." I found my reason and judgement suddenly absent presumed missing and became pulled along by their enthusiasm instead. The mystery was an unexpected excitement and a part of me was intrigued and wanted to find out what was going on. I just hoped Michael wasn't going to be stood waiting for us next to the windmill.

Firing up the Audi, I turned the heater on full blast and switched on the windscreen wipers to clear the snow that had started slowly falling once more. My hands filled with warmth as we drove along the quiet roads, the kids' excitement mounted, along with my fear, everyone else with an ounce of sense was indoors on a day like this. All too soon, we'd reached the little lay-by on the left, I pulled the car over and turned off the engine, wondering for the thousandth time if I was doing the right thing and wondering who would be waiting at the deserted windmill for us. There was no one around on account of the weather and we quietly walked up the little lane towards where the windmill stood, not knowing who would be waiting for us next to the little ticket office. "Look, look" Maddy had slightly run on ahead of us and was bouncing up and down in excitement. Tramping through the blanket of cold snow which covered our shins, it was a bit like trying to run in a dream, we soon caught up with her and looked at the door of the ticket office which was causing her much excitement, upon which we found another piece of paper with my name written on it, pinned to the door. I removed the gloves from my trembling hands and retrieved the note with a feeling of dread. It read, 'Come to the place where a Royal tried to make his escape.' "Oh this is ridiculous" I shouted into the empty fields. "Who does this to people ?"

"We've got to go to Carisbrooke Castle." Toby shouted over his shoulder as he marched back up the lane. "But how do you know ?" I chased his determined little form, clad in a warm winter coat and matching blue bobble hat. "We might not have actually visited half of this island yet, but I made sure that I thoroughly researched it before we moved. Charles the First was held in Carisbrooke Castle, before he was transported to London for his execution. While he was imprisoned at the castle he tried to escape out of his bedroom window."

"Can I go home and change into my Knight's costume before we go to the castle ?" The power ranger asked hopefully. "There's no time" shouted Toby before I could answer, "we can't let someone else find the next clue can we ?" I didn't want Maddy to try and escape again, after Michael's refusal to let her change her costume, so I tried a little damage limitation, "we're not going around the castle today honey, it's closed, but next time we go, I'll let you know before we leave and you can wear your full knight's outfit okay honey ?" The prospect of another visit seemed to mollify her, there was a way of dealing with Maddy and saying an outright 'no' was the worst reply you could give her and although I hadn't agreed to go back home, she was still happy. Michael had never understood the difference that a flexible approach made.

The weak wintry sun had given up its fight against the early encroaching darkness and I longed for a cup of hot coffee and my own fireside, but there was no way that I'd be allowed to give up the hunt now, so much to my own disbelief I found myself driving through Ashey, over the downs where the fields as far as the eye could see were covered in a thick white blanket, through Blackwater and finally up the steep hill to Carisbrooke Castle. The little green and red traffic light on a black and white pole made us wait for a few maddening minutes even though there was nothing likely to be coming the other way at dusk, with the road covered in snow, but I waited obediently anyway, Toby wouldn't forgive me if I was reckless. Was our mystery tormentor waiting just around the bend out of sight ?

Finally we pulled up outside the gateway entrance to the castle, which was firmly locked by a padlock with a sturdy looking combination lock. "Look it's there" shouted Toby, leaping out of the car and grabbing the little note secured to the gate with a piece of string. "I believe it's got my name on it, thank you." I didn't like the sinister feel I was getting from this lonely, snowy wild goose chase that some faceless psychopath was leading us on. Perhaps I should be calling the police instead of driving around the island, late on New Year's Eve with the kids in tow. 'One of the most curious things I've found on the Isle of Wight, are the needles that you can't thread.' Toby opened his mouth "yes thank you Toby, even I can work this one out."

The kids were even more excited as they jumped back into the car, but my stomach was beginning to rumble in protest, I hadn't even had lunch. I was determined that the drive to Alum Bay was to be the last, if we got there only to find another clue, I was going home and if someone was there waiting for us, then I was going to give them a piece of my mind, they'd be the ones calling the police after I'd finished with them. There was a bottle of merlot on the dining room table with my name on it and I didn't appreciate being kept away from it. Toby had spent most of the journey sending texts to Melody and I itched to find out what was making him giggle, but I had to respect his privacy, at least until he fell asleep and I could snoop through his phone. I was proud of him for finding someone, bless him, he'd never had a girlfriend at his last school, which was surely a good sign. Twenty five minutes later we were driving through the picturesque little village of Totland towards The Needles. I had vague memories of coming here as a child with my family. My mother had always loved looking at The Needles, the stacks of chalk towering out of the water, my father loved the battery and we would always end up at the little shop, filling small bottles with coloured sand. The roads had been quite empty up until now, but suddenly the traffic had started to build up and there were headlights everywhere, all making their way to the same destination as us. We followed the flow of cars and parked in the little car park overlooking The Needles themselves. "There must be something going on" I murmured. "Let's go down and find out where the next clue is" said Cassidy, slipping her small, warm gloved hand in mine. "Come on slowcoaches" shouted Maddy as she ran on slightly ahead of us as always. The park had changed a lot since my early childhood, which was more years ago than I cared to admit and as we walked through the gateway I was busy marvelling at all the attractions, there was glass blowing shop, funfair, sweet making shop, 4D cinema and a gift shop, there was more but it was hard to make out in the throng of tightly pressed people. I was so engrossed that I didn't even notice a man in a hooded jacket who stood blocking my way. "Hi Natasha." In the darkness it was impossible to make out a face and with all the noise I couldn't hear whether his voice was friendly or threatening. My heart was in my mouth and every instinct in me was telling me to run away, as he pulled his hood down to reveal, a smiling, very friendly face. "Mr Matthews," Cassidy breathed.

"Was it you leaving the clues ?" Toby asked, finally putting two and two together.

"Yes Toby, I wanted to surprise you all. Come on, follow me." I was glad the children were doing all the talking, because for once in my life I was completely and utterly speechless. Why had Dave come up with this elaborate plan, when he was in a relationship ? Had he wanted to do something to cheer the kids up ? If that was the case, I'd rather he'd have bought them a board game than drag us all across this frozen island. I followed behind them, until we got to a little café, inside one table at the back had a reserved sign on it, along with a long stemmed red rose and a candle burning brightly. Dave waved cheerily to the owner, who he obviously knew and led us to the quiet little table. "Why are there so many people here tonight ?" Toby fired at Dave, whilst scanning the laminated menu (who said that men can't multitask.) "It's the New Year's Eve fireworks, it's a bit of a tradition on the island, I was hoping it would be a bit quieter because of the weather, to be honest." Instantly, Maddy slammed her hands over her ears. "I don't like fireworks, they're too loud." Her cheeks were red and her bottom lip was trembling, she was close to tears at only the mention of fireworks, I was going to have to get her away from the park before the display started, I'd forgotten my handbag with her ear defenders in. "Good job I got these then." Dave pulled out three pairs of child's ear defenders, like some sort of lovely, amazing magician, making the kids' faces light up instantly, they couldn't wait to try them on and sat there in the middle of the café with their defenders snugly fitted, looking like three little Cheshire cats. Their inability to hear as well as normal, afforded me the perfect opportunity to speak to him without being interrupted, at least for a few minutes, until the novelty of the ear defenders wore off. "What's all this about Dave ? I'm confused ?" I hadn't even removed my coat or hat, just in case we had to leave at any given moment. "I couldn't understand what you meant the other night, when you said that Carole told you about Tristan, just as I was leaving." My cheeks started to flame in embarrassment and I looked at the kids, but they were busy pointing to various things they wanted to order, in some bizarre mime routine. "I just wanted you to know that I knew about him, that was all." I was mortified, had he really led me all across the island to tell me this, in front of the kids ? "It took ages for me to track Carole down that's why I haven't been in touch, I had to call in a few favours from colleagues to find out where she lived. She's not on Facebook sadly, but one of the ladies who works in the school reception could

lose her job if it came out that she helped me." He looked a bit sheepish, but a little bit proud, like a schoolboy who knew he'd done something wrong but was secretly proud of himself and couldn't resist bragging about it. "Oh no, you didn't have a go at her because of me did you ?" I felt the blood drain from my face, Carole was going to kill me. "Sort of, but don't worry, she's full of apologies." I wished desperately that I was at home with my bottle of merlot. "Tristan is my brother Natasha. We're really close, especially since his divorce last year and we always go on golfing holidays together." My brain moved slowly, but I was starting to fit the pieces of the jigsaw together. "So you weren't going clubbing ?"
"Erm no, we use golf CLUBS."
"But Carole said... Why would she say that ?" This conversation was getting crazier by the minute, I pinched myself under the table, to assure myself that I wasn't dreaming, but no, it was surreal, but it was actually happening. "Because I turned her down once at a works night out and she wasn't all that happy about it." None of this was making sense, but then I thought of the look on Carole's face when she'd told me and I could suddenly believe her of such slyness. "I wanted to ask you out and in truth I missed you that's why I phoned you on Christmas Eve, but I thought you weren't interested and then when you said that about Carole, it explained everything. Carole told me what she'd told you, she's mortified."
"Mummy I'm hungry." I could always depend on one of the kids to interrupt an important conversation. "Right, what would you like ?" Ten minutes later, we sat at the table, surrounded by

milkshakes, hot dogs and fries, the kids were so happy with their ear defenders, they insisted on keeping them on whilst they ate. "This is all very kind of you," I smiled, unable to believe the recent turn of events, my life was anything except boring. Maybe I wasn't destined to be a lonely old woman after all. "You've had a horrible time lately and I wanted to do something nice for you and the kids." After their father, had shown that he had no interest in them, it made my heart melt to know that this gorgeous, kind, caring man, didn't see my children as annoying baggage, he was actively involving them from the start, of whatever this was the beginning of. "There's just one other thing that I don't understand ?" I declared, waving my half eaten hot dog around in the air, "go on" he replied, his dreamy smile still on his perfect face. "Why the Keats and Tennyson poetry books ?" "Island poets are going to be our class topic next term and I thought you might want to read some of the poems in case the kids ask you about them. There's a particularly beautiful sonnet Keats wrote whilst in Shanklin and Tennyson's Enoch Arden is really sad, but beautiful too, he wrote it here on the island. I thought you might be in need of a little romance at the moment." He was right there, it had been a long time since I'd experienced any romance. "How on earth are you single ?" I hadn't meant to ask him outright, but now that I had, I was curious to find out what he would say. "It's a bit cliché, but I was ready to settle down and my ex wasn't. I was happy here on the island, but it was too small a place for her. We split up about eight months ago, last I heard she was working as a holiday rep in Ibiza and I threw myself into my work." This was all sounding promising, but I had to make sure we were suited. "Dave, do you like old eighties and nineties films like Casper?" He chuckled, but for once there was a man laughing with me and not at me. "Are you kidding, I love that film, Tristan and I used to watch it all the time when we were kids. Have you ever seen the old Goldie Hawn and Kurt Russell film Overboard?" I nodded, captivated by this perfect man. "Well Kurt Russell's pick up truck was the same one they used in National Lampoon's Christmas Vacation, you know the one that Chevy Chase drives under the lorry?" It was all I could do not to snog him in the middle of the café with everyone watching, but I thought of how mortified the kids would be and decided against it.

Just as the food and drink were demolished, loud booms sounded in the air signalling that the fireworks had begun. Putting on our coats, we took the children out among the crowds of people who'd come to start the New Year festivities off with an early firework display for the kids. As I stood, watching the spectacle, Dave slipped a hand into mine and we stood like a real family. I didn't want to rush things, but the New Year was definitely looking up.

A word from the Author

Apart from my family, the other things that I love most in the world are the Isle of Wight and Christmas and I couldn't think of anything more enjoyable to write about, than these two subjects combined. It's just a little thing, but as I wanted to keep as much authenticity in this book as possible and stay as true to my beloved Isle of Wight and its wonderful places as I can, I just felt that I needed to point out to you good reader, that apart from the characters in this story, the only times (in this story) where I've told little white lies, start with the fact that according to Google, there are no such places as 'St Cuthbert's Primary School' or 'Peter Pan's Pre-School' on the Isle of Wight. The reason for choosing these fictional names is that these settings and the staff are important features in this book and I didn't want to cast any aspersions on the existing schools and the great staff who work in them. Also, as far as I'm aware there isn't a little café at The Needles park, (though I really think there should be for the amount of visitors they get) and also, The Needles don't have Firework Displays on New Year's Eve, so I hope you'll permit me some artistic licence and I hope it doesn't mean that Santa puts me on the naughty list this year.

I have two children who are diagnosed with Asperger's Syndrome and Pathological Demand Avoidance and all children who are on the spectrum differ vastly from one another, but I hope that I managed to at least convey a little of what it is like to have children with this invisible disability, though a lot of parents and carers are dealing with far more severe traits than the characters in my book and although Michael is at the extreme end of fatherhood, I want to stress that there are some amazing daddies out there who do a fantastic job raising their children. In my desire to read Autism related fiction, most of the stories I read were about children on the spectrum whose mother's couldn't cope with their children and had left them with their father and walked out, so I wanted to balance this a little. I recently heard a very sad report that parents of children with Autism and PDA in particular, have the highest divorce rates, luckily that part of the book wasn't based on my own experience, but is drawn from that of many, many friends of mine who have children on the spectrum whose partners just couldn't cope with the fact that their children weren't what they hoped for, luckily most of these friends have also gone on to find love, with good supportive men who have really stepped up to being amazing stepfathers.

I hope you enjoyed it and Happy Christmas,

Sarah

About the Author

Sarah Sprules lives in the South West of England with her husband and two children who have both been diagnosed with Asperger's Syndrome and Pathological Demand Avoidance Syndrome.
When she isn't actually visiting the Isle of Wight, Sarah likes to write books about the island, to pass the time until she can visit once more. Sarah writes historical novels as well as those dealing with children on the spectrum.

You can contact Sarah via:-
Twitter, @Sprulesy1
Facebook, www.facebook.com/sarahsscriptorium
Email, sarahsscriptorium@fsmail.net

Made in the USA
Charleston, SC
20 August 2015